TOP JAVA CHALLENGES: CRACKING THE CODING INTERVIEW

Based on 30 real questions

Moises Gamio

Top Java Challenge: Cracking the Coding Interview

by Moises Gamio
Copyright © 2020 Moises Gamio. All rights reserved.

No part of this book may be reproduced, or stored in a retrieval system, or transmitted in any form or by any means, electronic, mechanical, photocopying, recording, or otherwise, without express written permission of the publisher.

If you find any error in the text or the code or if you have any suggestions, please let me know by emailing at support@codersite.dev. Once you have read and used this book, please leave a review on the site that you purchased it. By doing so, you can help me improve the next editions of this book. Thanks, and I hope you enjoy using the text in your job interview!

Cover designer: Maria Elena Gamio

ISBN: 9798650252368

For Lorena

Contents

PREFACE	vi
1. Reverse a Text	1
2. Validate a leap year	4
3. Given an integer N, returns the smallest number	6
4. Fizz Buzz	8
5. Sum of all even numbers from 1 to a given Integer	10
6. Validate if a string has all unique characters	11
7. Validate if a string is a Palindrome	13
8. Verify if a number is a valid power of a base	15
9. Checking if a number is Prime	17
10. Distance between two points	19
11. Write an immutable Class to convert currencies	21
12. Compare application version numbers	24
13. Reverse a linked list	26
14. Remove duplicates from a list	29
15. Given an integer N, returns its Factorial	31
16. Bubble Sort	33
17. Insertion Sort	36
18. Quick Sort	38
19. Binary Search	40
20. Rotate the matrix by 90 degrees	42
21. Delimiter Matching	44
22. Queue via Stacks	46
23. Number of products of two consecutive integers	48
24. Return the most frequent elements of an array	50
25. Assemble Parts in minimum Time	52
26. Binary Search Tree	54
27. Depth-First Search (DFS)	59
28. Breadth-First Search (BFS)	68
29. Optimize online purchases	73
30. Tic tac toe	81
Appendices	101
A. Big O Notation	102

PREFACE

I am a software engineer who faced real interviews as a candidate for startups and big companies. Throughout the years, I have sourced factual questions that have been tried, tested, and commented on step by step and are now part of this book!. I hope you find them practical and useful in your career search.

The job market is tough, and everyday big firms and tech startups receive many applicants, where the need to filter the best one becomes a daunting process. Yes, your CV matters. The interview by phone and the code challenge to be solved at home will lead you to the last and most decisive stage of the recruiting process, where the interviewer evaluates your problem-solving skills and knowledge of efficient data structures and algorithms.

Usually, the interviewer poses a complex problem to solve in a limited time. You need to provide rationales about design choices made in your proposed solution in terms of resource and time efficiency.

Therefore, knowing the most appropriate data structures and algorithms to solve common problems that frequently are used in the recruiting process can be a decisive factor. Whether your knowledge of efficient data structures and algorithms is scarce or buried in your memory since you learned about them for the first time, this book can help you. It includes the most common questions, and their respective solutions, that you can find in a real interview. Recall, the more prepared you are, the more points you accumulate in an objective way with respect to other candidates.

This book includes typical questions based on real interviews that you must know and practice. All solved and explained in detail.

Typical questions include String manipulation, arrays, variables swapping, linked list, refactoring, recursion, sorting, searching, stacks, queues, trees, graphs, optimization, and games. In these questions you can see how to choose the right data structure for their optimal implementation.

Also included are questions where you can design an algorithm based on the test development-driven approach, which is extremely essential for the companies of today.

The more prepared and confident you are, the better the chances of negotiating your next salary.

Moises Gamio
Software Engineer, Senior Java Developer

1. Reverse a Text

Given a string of characters, reverse the order of the characters in an efficient manner.

Solution

We choose an **array** – holds values of a single type - as our data structure because the algorithm receives a small amount of data, which is predictable and is read it randomly (its numerical index accesses each element).

Firstly, convert the text to be reversed, to a character array. Then, calculate the length of the string.

Secondly, swap the position of array elements using a loop. Don't use additional memory, which means avoiding unnecessary objects or variables (space complexity). Swapping does it in-place by transposing values using a temporary variable. Then, swap the first element with the last, the second element with the penultimate, and so on. Moreover, we only need to iterate until half of the array.

Finally, it returns the new character array as a String. Listing 1.1 shows the algorithm.

Listing 1.1 - Reverse a Text

```java
public class StringUtils {
  public static String reverse(String text) {
    char[] chars =text.toCharArray();
    final int arrayLength =chars.length;
    char temp;
    for (int idx =0; idx < arrayLength/2; idx++) {
      temp =chars[idx];
      chars[idx] =chars[arrayLength - 1 - idx];
      chars[arrayLength - 1 - idx] =temp;
    }
    return String.valueOf(chars);
  }
}
```

Example:

When idx = 0:
chars = {a, b, c, 2, 1, 3, 2}

```
chars[idx] = a
chars[arrayLength-1-idx] = 2

When idx = 1:
chars = {2, b, c, 2, 1, 3, a}
chars[idx] = b
chars[arrayLength-1-idx] = 3

When idx = 2:
chars = {2, 3, c, 2, 1, b, a}
chars[idx] = c
chars[arrayLength-1-idx] = 1

When idx = 3:
chars = {2, 3, 1, 2, c, b, a}
idx is not less than arrayLength/2
end
```

Tests

```
@Test
public void reverseText_useCases() {
    assertEquals("abc2132", StringUtils.reverse("2312cba"));
    assertEquals("ba", StringUtils.reverse("ab"));
}
```

During the interview, it is common to receive additional questions about your code. For instance, what happens if we pass a *null* argument.

To avoid a NullPointerException, we need to add the following precondition:

```
if (text == null)
    throw new RuntimeException("text is not initialized");
```

```
@Test(expected = RuntimeException.class)
public void reverseText_exceptionThrownCase() {
    assertEquals("cda1", StringUtils.reverse(null));
}
```

Moreover, the interviewer wants our algorithm to reverse only those characters, which occupy an odd position inside of the array. The % operator is used to detect these locations.

Under the *loop for* sentence, we need to add the following conditional sentence:

```
if ((idx+1) % 2 != 0) {
  ...
```

```
@Test
public void reverseOdssText() {
  assertEquals("ub32tca192", StringUtils.reverse ("2b12cta39u"));
}
```

What is the performance of the algorithm?

Start to analyze the most important sentences:

```
char[] chars =text.toCharArray();     -> runs in only 1 execution: O(1)
final int arrayLength =chars.length;  -> runs in only 1 execution: O(1)
for (int idx=0; idx<arrayLength/2; idx++){  -> runs in O(N)
return String.valueOf(chars);         -> runs in only 1 execution: O(1)
```

Total time: O(1) + O(1) + O(N) + O(1) = O(N)

In this scenario, A constant time O(1) is insignificance compared with a linear time O(N)

See appendix A find out why Big O Notation ignores constants

For instance:

When `chars.length` is 100, then,
Total time:
O(1)+O(1)+O(100/2)+O(1) = 1+1+50+1 = 53 ≈ 50 → (N/2) → N

When `chars.length` is 100000, then,
Total time:
O(1)+O(1)+O(100000/2)+O(1) = 1+1+50000+1 = 50003 ≈ 50000 → (N/2) → N

Therefore, we can say that our Reverse Text algorithm runs in O(N) time.

2. Validate a leap year

A **leap year** is a calendar year containing an additional day. This extra day occurs in February. The following rules define a leap year:

- A year will be a leap year if it is divisible by 4, but not by 100

  or

- A year will be a leap if it is divisible by 400.

Solution

We use the % operator to verify if a year is divisible by 4, 100, or 400. Listing 2.1 shows the algorithm.

Listing 2.1 - Validate a leap year

```java
public class IsLeapYear implements Function<Integer, Boolean> {

  @Override
  public Boolean apply(Integer number) {
    return isLeapYear(number);
  }

  private static boolean isLeapYear(int year) {
    return (year % 400 == 0) ||
           (year % 4 == 0 && year % 100 != 0);
  }
}
```

This algorithm had a real application in the Y2K problem, where COBOL programs in a Bank used to store four-digits years with only the final **two digits,** so you could not distinguish 2000 from 1900. In addition to calculating a leap year:

For years represented from 50 until 99, add 19 at begin, so it results in 1950 until 1999.
For years represented from 00 until 49, add 20 at begin, so it results in 2000 until 2049.

The Bank assumed that before 2049 all systems would be migrated to modern programming languages (digital transformation), but that is another story.

Tests

```java
public class IsLeapYearTest {

    private IsLeapYear isLeapYear;

    @Before
    public void before() {
        isLeapYear = new IsLeapYear();
    }

    @Test
    public void isLeapYear() {
        assertTrue(isLeapYear.apply(400));
        assertTrue(isLeapYear.apply(2000));
        assertTrue(isLeapYear.apply(2020));
    }

    @Test
    public void is_notLeapYear() {
        assertFalse(isLeapYear.apply(401));
        assertFalse(isLeapYear.apply(2018));
    }
}
```

3. Given an integer N, returns the smallest number

Write a method that, given an original number *N* of *d* digits, returns the smallest number with the same number of digits. For example, given N=4751, the method should return to 1000. Given N=1, the method should return 0.

Solution

Maybe the first idea that comes to our minds could be to iterate from the given number and decrease one by one, and in every iteration to check if every new number contains one digit less than the original number. If the answer is True, then the previous one is the smallest number with the same number of digits of the original number. Listing 3.1 shows the first algorithm.

First solution:

Listing 3.1 - Given an integer N, returns the smallest number

```java
public class NumberUtils {
  public static int smallest(int N) {
    int smallestNumber = 0;
    if (N <= 1)
      return smallestNumber;

    int numberOfDigitsOriginalN = String.valueOf(N).length();
    while (N > 0) {
      N--;
      if (String.valueOf(N).length() ==
          (numberOfDigitsOriginalN -1)) {
        return ++N;
      }
    }
    return smallestNumber;
  }
}
```

But If we realize, the solution follows a particular pattern:

N = 4751 -> smallest number = 1000
N = 189 -> smallest number = 100
N = 37 -> smallest number = 10

The smallest number is a power of 10, where the exponent is: *number of digits – 1*

Better solution:

Listing 3.2 – Given an integer N, returns the smallest number

```java
public class NumberUtils {
  public static int smallest(int N) {
    int smallestNumber = 0;
    if (N <= 1 || String.valueOf(N).length() == 1) {
      return smallestNumber;
    }
    int numberOfDigits = String.valueOf(N).length();
    return (int) Math.pow(10, numberOfDigits - 1);
  }
}
```

The main idea in Analysis of Algorithms is always to improve the algorithm performance by reducing the number of steps and comparisons. The simpler and more intuitive an algorithm is, the more useful and efficient it will be.

Tests

```java
public class SmallestNumberTest {

  @Test
  public void test_right_smallest_values() {
    assertTrue(NumberUtils.smallest(4751) == 1000);
    assertTrue(NumberUtils.smallest(189) == 100);
    assertTrue(NumberUtils.smallest(37) == 10);
    assertTrue(NumberUtils.smallest(1) == 0);
  }

  @Test
  public void test_wrong_smallest_values() {
    assertFalse(NumberUtils.smallest(8) == 1);
    assertFalse(NumberUtils.smallest(2891) == 2000);
  }
}
```

4. Fizz Buzz

Write a program that will display all the numbers between 1 and 100.

- For each number divisible by three the program will display the word "Fizz."
- For each number divisible by five the program will display the word "Buzz."
- For each number divisible by three and by five the program will display the word "Fizz-Buzz."

The output will look like:

1, 2, Fizz, 4, Buzz, Fizz, 7, 8, Fizz, Buzz, 11, Fizz, 13, 14, Fizz-Buzz, 16, 19, ...

Solution

It looks a simple algorithm but is "hard" for some programmers because they try to follow the following reasoning:

```
if (theNumber is divisible by 3) then
    print "Fizz"
else if (theNumber is divisible by 5) then
    print "Buzz"
else /* theNumber is not divisible by 3 or 5 */
    print theNumber
end if
```

But where do we print "Fizz-Buzz" in this algorithm?. The interviewer expects that you think for yourself and made good use of conditional without duplication. Realizing that a number divisible by 3 and 5 is also divisible by 3*5 is the key to a FizzBuzz solution. Listing 4.1 shows the algorithm.

Listing 4.1 – Fizz Buzz

```java
public class NumberUtils {

  public static void fizzBuzz(int N) {
    final String BUZZ = "Buzz";
    final String FIZZ = "Fizz";

    for (int i = 1; i <= N; i++) {
```

```java
      if (i % 15 == 0) {
        System.out.print(FIZZ + "-" + BUZZ + ", ");
      } else if (i % 3 == 0) {
        System.out.print(FIZZ + ", ");
      } else if (i % 5 == 0) {
        System.out.print(BUZZ + ", ");
      } else {
        System.out.print(i + ", ");
      }
    }
  }
}
```

You should never use `System.out.print` in a Production environment. I/O routines consume a lot of resources in time and memory.

Tests

```java
public class FizzBuzzTest {

  @Test
  public void testFizzBuzz() {
    NumberUtils.fizzBuzz(100);
  }
}
```

5. Sum of all even numbers from 1 to a given Integer

Given an Integer *N*, calculates the sum all even numbers from 1 to *N*.

Solution

It looks like an easy program, but believe me, most experienced programmers during the interview forget to use the operator "%," which returns the division remainder. If it is 0, the number is even; otherwise, it is odd. Listing 5.1 shows the algorithm.

Listing 5.1 – Sum of all even numbers from 1 to N

```java
public class SumOfEvenNumbers implements Function<Integer, Integer> {

  @Override
  public Integer apply(Integer N) {
    int sum = 0;
    for (int number = 1; number <= N; number++)
      if ((number % 2) == 0)
        sum = sum + number;

    return sum;
  }
}
```

Tests

```java
@Test
public void sumOfEvenNumbers_test() {
  assertEquals(42, sumOfEvenNumbers.apply(12).intValue());
  assertEquals(110, sumOfEvenNumbers.apply(21).intValue());
}
```

6. Validate if a string has all unique characters

Given a string of characters, validate if all of them are unique.

Solution

We assume the charset is ASCII. Originally based on the English alphabet, **ASCII** encodes 128 specified **characters** into seven-bit integers. Ninety-five of the encoded **characters** are printable: these include the digits *0* to *9*, lowercase letters *a* to *z*, uppercase letters *A* to *Z*, and punctuation symbols.

Firstly, create a Boolean array to store the occurrence of every character

Secondly, iterate the String of characters, use the java *charAt* method to return the numerical representation for every character. Check this value in the Boolean array. If it exists, then the String has not unique values. Otherwise, store this value in the Boolean array as its first occurrence.

Finally, if all characters had only one occurrence in the Boolean array, then the String has all unique characters. Listing 6.1 shows the algorithm.

```
Listing 6.1 - Validate if a String has all unique characters

import java.util.function.Function;

public class AreUniqueChars implements Function<String, Boolean> {

  @Override
  public Boolean apply(String str) {
    return areUniqueChars(str);
  }

  static boolean areUniqueChars(String str) {
    if (str.length() > 128)
      return false;

    boolean[] booleans = new boolean[128];
    for (int idx = 0; idx < str.length(); idx++) {
      int value = str.charAt(idx);
      if (booleans[value]) { //is found?
        return false;
      }
```

```java
      booleans[value] = true;
    }
    return true;
  }
}
```

Tests

```java
public class AreUniqueCharsTest {

  AreUniqueChars areUniqueChars;

  @Before
  public final void setup() {
    areUniqueChars = new AreUniqueChars();
  }

  @Test
  public void is_not_UniqueChars() {
    assertFalse(areUniqueChars.apply("29s2"));
    assertFalse(areUniqueChars.apply("1903aio9p"));
  }

  @Test
  public void is_UniqueChars() {
    assertTrue(areUniqueChars.apply("29s13"));
    assertTrue(areUniqueChars.apply("2813450769"));
  }
}
```

7. Validate if a string is a Palindrome

A **palindrome** is a string that reads the same forward and backward, for example, level, wow, and madam.

Solution

We can loop through each character and check it against another one on the opposite side. If one of these checks fails, then the text is not Palindrome. Listing 7.1 shows the algorithm.

Listing 7.1 – Validate if a String is a Palindrome

```java
import java.util.function.Function;

public class IsPalindrome implements Function<String, Boolean> {

  @Override
  public Boolean apply(String text) {
    return isPalindrome(text);
  }

  static boolean isPalindrome(String text) {
    final int length = text.length();
    for (int idx = 0; idx < length / 2; idx++) {
      if (text.charAt(idx) != text.charAt(length - 1 - idx))
        return false;
    }
    return true;
  }
}
```

Tests

```java
public class IsPalindromeTest {

  private IsPalindrome isPalindrome;

  @Before
  public final void before() {
    isPalindrome = new IsPalindrome();
  }
  @Test
```

```java
    public void is_not_palindrome() {
        assertFalse(isPalindrome.apply("2f1"));
        assertFalse(isPalindrome.apply("-101"));
    }

    @Test
    public void is_palindrome() {
        assertTrue(isPalindrome.apply("2f1f2"));
        assertTrue(isPalindrome.apply("-101-"));
        assertTrue(isPalindrome.apply("9"));
        assertTrue(isPalindrome.apply("99"));
        assertTrue(isPalindrome.apply("madam"));
    }
}
```

8. Verify if a number is a valid power of a base

Exponentiation involves two numbers, the base *b,* and the exponent or power *n.* Exponentiation corresponds to repeated multiplication of the base *n* times. For instance, in the following expression: $3^5 = 243$, we say that 243 is the *5th* power of 3. Therefore, 243 is the correct power of 3.

Solution

In mathematics, a function is an expression that maps an independent variable (domain) to a dependent variable (range). Functional programming (FP) emphasizes functions that produce results that depend **only on their inputs and not on the program state**—i.e., pure mathematical functions.

One of Java's approaches to FP is the definition of functional interfaces. A functional interface in Java is one that has only one abstract method. We can use functional components available in the Java 8 library like the `java.util.function.BiFunction<T, U, R>`, which accepts two arguments and produces one result.

To verify if a number is a valid power *nth* of another number (*base*), we do the inverse operation.
Implementing the behavior of the *apply* method: divide the given number by the *base* and evaluate if it provides a 0 remainder, then we iterate this operation until we find a value of 1. Otherwise, if the rest is not 0, then the given number is not a valid *power nth* of the *base*. Listing 8.1 shows a function, which returns true when a given number is the right power of a base.

Listing 8.1 - Verify if a number is a valid power of a base

```java
public class IsNumberAValidPowerOfBase implements BiFunction<Integer, Integer, Boolean> {

  @Override
  public Boolean apply(Integer number, Integer base) {
    return isNumberAValidPowerOfBase(number, base);
  }

  static boolean isNumberAValidPowerOfBase(int number, int base) {
    if (number == 0)
```

```java
      return true;

    while (number != 1) {
      if ((number % base) != 0)
        return false;

      number = number / base;
    }
    return true;
  }
}
```

Tests

```java
public class IsNumberAValidPowerOfBaseTest {
  private IsNumberAValidPowerOfBase isNumberAValidPowerOfBase;

  @Before
  public void before() {
    isNumberAValidPowerOfBase = new IsNumberAValidPowerOfBase();
  }

  @Test
  public void testOfWrongReturnValues() {
    assertFalse(isNumberAValidPowerOfBase.apply(6, 2));
    assertFalse(isNumberAValidPowerOfBase.apply(16, 5));
    assertFalse(isNumberAValidPowerOfBase.apply(14, 7));
  }

  @Test
  public void testOfValidReturnValues() {
    assertTrue(isNumberAValidPowerOfBase.apply(243, 3));
    assertTrue(isNumberAValidPowerOfBase.apply(16, 4));
    assertTrue(isNumberAValidPowerOfBase.apply(125, 5));
  }
}
```

9. Checking if a number is Prime

A prime number is a whole number greater than one, whose only factors are one and itself. A factor is a whole number that can be divided evenly into another number. For instance: 2, 3, 5, 7, 11 are prime numbers.

Solution

A simple solution is to iterate decreasingly through all numbers from the half of the given number *n*, and for every number, check if it divides *n*. If we find any number that divides, then we return false. Otherwise, it returns true. Listing 9.1 shows the algorithm.

Listing 9.1 - Checking if a number is Prime.

```java
import java.util.function.Function;

public class IsPrimeNumber implements Function<Integer, Boolean> {

  @Override
  public Boolean apply(Integer number) {
    return isPrimeNumber(number);
  }

  private static boolean isPrimeNumber(int number) {
    if (number < 2)
      return false;

    if (number == 2)
      return true;

    for (int div = (number / 2) + 1; div > 1; div--) {
      if (number % div == 0) {
        return false;
      }
    }
    return true;
  }
}
```

Tests

```java
public class IsPrimeNumberTest {
  IsPrimeNumber;

  @Before
  public void setup() {
    isPrimeNumber = new IsPrimeNumber();
  }
  @Test
  public void notPrimeNumbers() {
    assertFalse(isPrimeNumber.apply(-1));
    assertFalse(isPrimeNumber.apply(625));
    assertFalse(isPrimeNumber.apply(4));
    assertFalse(isPrimeNumber.apply(100));
  }

  @Test
  public void primeNumbers() {
    assertTrue(isPrimeNumber.apply(2));
    assertTrue(isPrimeNumber.apply(3));
    assertTrue(isPrimeNumber.apply(5));
    assertTrue(isPrimeNumber.apply(7));
    assertTrue(isPrimeNumber.apply(73));
  }
}
```

10. Distance between two points

Given two points, calculate the distance between them.

Solution

Each Point has coordinates *(x,y)*, so we can calculate the distance with the hypotenuse. Listing 10.1 shows the algorithm.

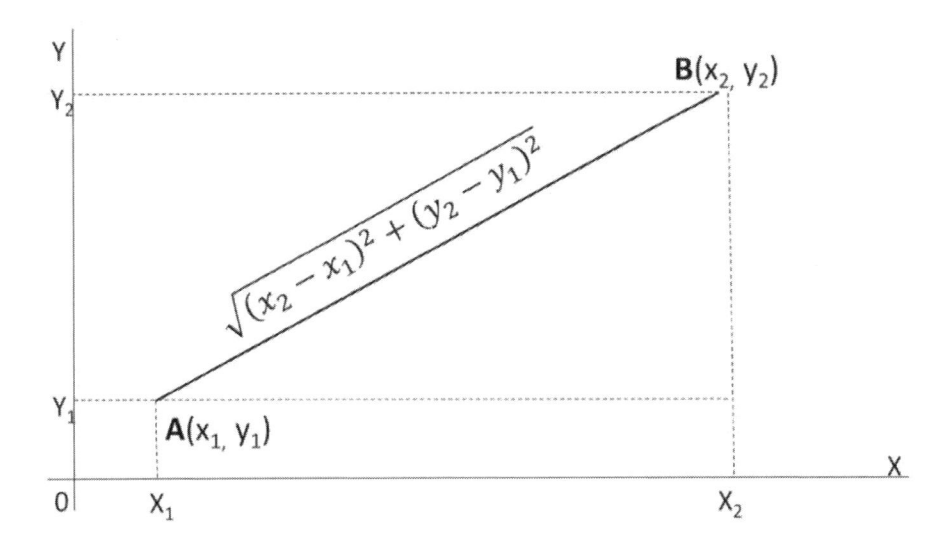

Figure 10.1 Distance between two points

Listing 10.1 - Distance between two points.

```
public class Point {
  final double x;
  final double y;

  public Point(double x, double y) {
    this.x = x;
    this.y = y;
  }

  public double distance(Point point) {
    if (this == null || point == null)
```

```java
      throw new RuntimeException("Points are not initialized");
    double dx = this.x - point.x;
    double dy = this.y - point.y;
    return Math.sqrt(dx * dx + dy * dy);
  }
}
```

Tests

```java
@Test
public void given_twoPoints_return_distance() {
  Point point1 = new Point(2, 3);
  Point point2 = new Point(5, 7);
  assertEquals(5, point1.distance(point2), 0);
}
```

Other useful methods included in the Math Class:

abs(x): Returns the absolute value of x.
abs(-1) = 1;
round(x): Returns the value of x rounded to its nearest integer.
round(4.4) = 4
ceil(x): Returns the value of x rounded up to its nearest integer.
ceil(4,4) = 5.0
floor(x): Returns the value of x rounded down to its nearest integer.
floor(4.4) = 4.0
max(x): Returns the number with the highest value.
max(6,7) = 7
pow(x,y): Returns the value of x to the power of y.
pow(2,5) = 32.0
random(): Returns a random number between 0 and 1.
random() => 0.45544344999209374

11. Write an immutable Class to convert currencies

Design a Money Class, which can convert Euros to Dollars and vice versa. As examples, write two instances with the following values: 67.89 EUR and 98.76 USD

Solution

An immutable class is a class whose instances cannot be modified. Its information is fixed for the lifetime of the object without changes.

To make a class immutable, we follow these rules:

- Don't include a mutators method that could modify the object's state.
- Don't allow to extend the class.
- Make all class members final and private
- Ensure exclusive access to any mutable components. Don't make references to those objects. Make defensive copies.

Immutable objects are thread-safe; they require no synchronization. For our class, we use a BigDecimal data type because it provides operations on numbers for arithmetic, rounding, and can handle large floating-point numbers with great precision. Listing 11.1 shows an immutable Class.

Listing 11.1 - Money Class

```java
import java.math.BigDecimal;

public final class Money {
  private static final String DOLAR = "USD";
  private static final String EURO = "EUR";
  private static int ROUNDING_MODE = BigDecimal.ROUND_HALF_EVEN;
  private static int DECIMALS = 2;
  private BigDecimal amount;
  private String currency;

  public Money() {}

  public static Money valueOf(
```

```java
      BigDecimal amount,
      String currency) {
    return new Money(amount, currency);
  }

  //Caller cannot see this private constructor
  private Money(
      BigDecimal amount,
      String currency) {
    this.amount = amount;
    this.currency = currency;
  }

  //Currency converter
  public Money multiply(BigDecimal factor) {
    return Money.valueOf(
        rounded(this.amount.multiply(factor)),
        this.currency.equals(DOLAR) ? EURO : DOLAR);
  }

  //round to 2 decimals
  private BigDecimal rounded(BigDecimal amount) {
    return amount.setScale(DECIMALS, ROUNDING_MODE);
  }

  public BigDecimal getAmount() {
    return amount;
  }

  public String getCurrency() {
    return currency;
  }
}
```

String class produces immutable objects, so we can trust in any client who passes it in the arguments. But this is not the case for BigDecimal, which can be extended and manipulated for some untrusted clients, e.g., to expand its toString() method.

java.math

Class BigDecimal

java.lang.Object
    java.lang.Number
        java.math.BigDecimal

All Implemented Interfaces:

    Serializable, Comparable<BigDecimal>

```
public class BigDecimal
extends Number
implements Comparable<BigDecimal>
```

To protect our class from untrusted clients we can create copies of these arguments. The following code shows the multiply method modified.

```java
//Currency converter, more secure
public Money multiplysecure(BigDecimal factor) {
  if (factor.getClass() == BigDecimal.class)
    factor = new BigDecimal(factor.toString());
  else {
    //TODO throw exception?
  }
  return Money.valueOf(
      rounded(this.amount.multiply(factor)),
      this.currency.equals(DOLAR) ? EURO : DOLAR);
}
```

Tests:

```java
public class MoneyTest {

  @Test
  public void convert_EURO_to_DOLLAR() {
    final Money moneyInEuros = Money.valueOf(
      new BigDecimal("67.89"), "EUR");
    final Money moneyInDollar = moneyInEuros
      .multiply(new BigDecimal("1.454706142288997"));
    assertEquals(new BigDecimal("98.76"),
      moneyInDollar.getAmount());
  }

  @Test
  public void convert_DOLLAR_to_EURO() {
    final Money moneyInDollar = Money.valueOf(
      new BigDecimal("98.76"), "USD");
    final Money moneyInEuros = moneyInDollar
      .multiply(new BigDecimal("0.6874240583232078"));
    assertEquals(new BigDecimal("67.89"),
      moneyInEuros.getAmount());
  }
}
```

12. Compare application version numbers

Semantic versioning is a formal convention for specifying compatibility using a three-part **version number**: major **version**, minor **version**, and patch. Minor changes and bug fixes increment the patch **number**, which does not change the software's **application** programming interface (API). Given version1 and version2, returns:

* -1 if version1 < version2
* 1 if version1 > version2
* 0 if version1 == version2

Solution

Firstly, we must split the version number into its components. Since the input is in the form of strings, there is a need to divide them, given the dot delimiter that separates them to convert them to int arrays.

Secondly, we must iterate the arrays while it has not achieved at least one of the lengths of the arrays. Compare each component from the left to the right side. In case that one version contains one more component than the other one, then check that a value of 0 in that additional component is not representative.

Finally, we return 0 (equals) when versions were not different during the iteration. Listing 12.1 shows the algorithm.

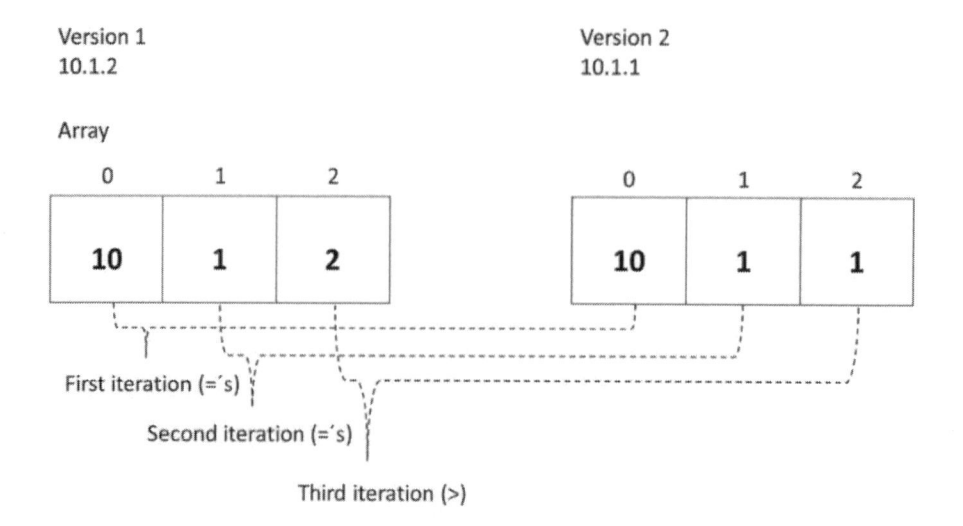

Figure 12.1 Compare application version numbers

Listing 12.1 - Compare application version numbers

```java
public class VersionNumber {
  public static int compare(String v1, String v2) {

    int[] a1 = Arrays.stream(v1.split("\\."))
      .map(String::trim)
      .mapToInt(Integer::parseInt).toArray();
    int[] a2 = Arrays.stream(v2.split("\\."))
      .map(String::trim)
      .mapToInt(Integer::parseInt).toArray();
    int idx = 0;
    while (idx < a1.length || idx < a2.length) {
      if (idx < a1.length && idx < a2.length) {
        if (a1[idx] < a2[idx]) {
          return -1;
        } else if (a1[idx] > a2[idx]) {
          return 1;
        }
      } else if (idx < a1.length) {
        if (a1[idx] != 0) {
          return 1;
        }
      } else if (idx < a2.length) {
        if (a2[idx] != 0) {
          return -1;
        }
      }
      idx++;
    }
    return 0;
  }
}
```

Tests

```java
@Test
public void versionNumber_usesCases() {
  assertEquals(0, VersionNumber.compare("15", "15.0"));
  assertEquals(0, VersionNumber.compare("10.1", "10.1.0"));
  assertEquals(-1, VersionNumber.compare("10.1", "10.1.1"));
  assertEquals(1, VersionNumber.compare("10.1.2", "10.1.1"));
}
```

13. Reverse a linked list

Given a pointer to the head node of a linked list, write a program to reverse the linked list.

Solution

Unlike arrays, linked list store items at a not contiguous location; It connects items using pointers. In a linked list, a node embeds data items. A node is an object of a class called something like Node. Because there are many similar nodes in a list, it makes sense to use a separate Class for them, distinct from the linked list itself. Each Node object contains a reference (usually called next) to the next node in the list. A field in the list itself contains a reference to the first node. Linked Lists utilize memory more effectively.

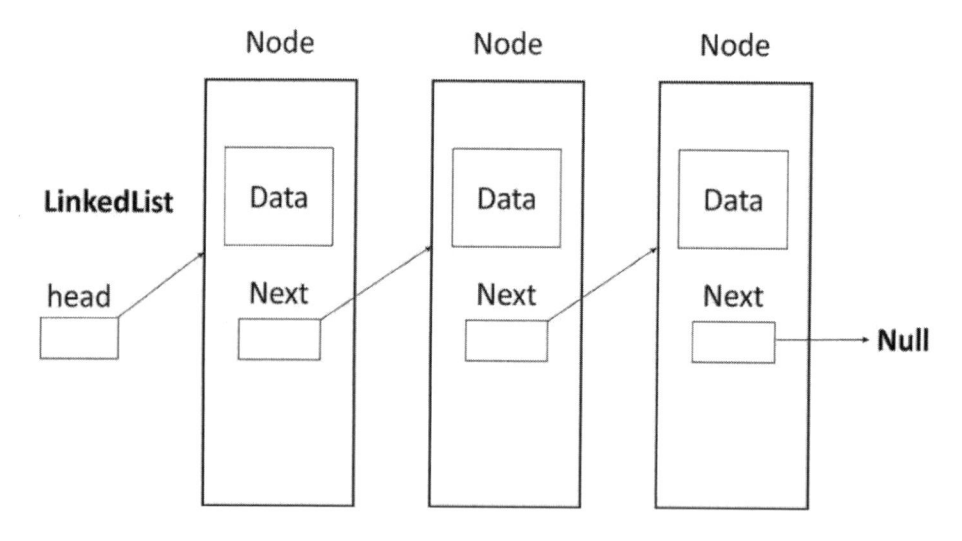

Figure 13.1 Linked List

To reverse a linked list, we implement an iterative method:

1. Initialize three-pointers: *prev* as NULL, *current* as head, and *next* as NULL.
2. Iterate through the linked list. In the loop, do the following:

    // Before changing *next* of *current*,
    // Store *next* node
    next = current->next

    // Now change *next* of *current*,
    // This is where actual reversing happens

```
current->next = prev
```

```
// Move prev and current one step forward
prev = current
current = next
```

Listing 13.1 shows a Generic LinkedList class with an *add* method and the reverse algorithm.

Listing 13.1 – Reverse a LinkedList

```java
import java.util.StringJoiner;

public class LinkedList<T> {
  Node head;

  private class Node {
    final T value;
    Node next;

    Node(T value, Node next) {
      this.value = value;
      this.next = next;
    }
  }

  public void add(T value) {
    Node node = new Node(value, null);
    if (head == null) {
      head = node;
    } else {
      Node last = head;
      while (last.next != null) {
        last = last.next;
      }
      last.next = node;
    }
  }

  @Override
  public String toString() {
    StringJoiner stringJoiner = new StringJoiner(" -> ", "[", "]");
    Node last = head;
    while (last != null) {
      stringJoiner.add(last.value.toString());
      last = last.next;
    }
    return stringJoiner.toString();
```

```java
  }
  public void reverse() {
    if (head == null)
      return;

    Node prev = null;
    Node current = head;
    Node next = null;
    while (current != null) {
      next = current.next;
      current.next = prev;
      prev = current;
      current = next;
    }
    head = prev;
  }
}
```

Tests

```java
@Test
public void reverseLinkedList() {
  LinkedList<String> linkedList = new LinkedList<>();
  linkedList.add("s1"); linkedList.add("s2");
  linkedList.add("s3"); linkedList.add("s4");
  linkedList.reverse();
  assertEquals("[s4 -> s3 -> s2 -> s1]",
      linkedList.toString());
}

@Test
public void reverseIntegersLinkedList() {
  LinkedList<Integer> linkedList = new LinkedList<>();
  linkedList.add(new Integer(1));
  linkedList.add(new Integer(2));
  linkedList.add(new Integer(5));
  linkedList.reverse();
  assertEquals("[5 -> 2 -> 1]", linkedList.toString());
}
```

14. Remove duplicates from a list

Write a program to check if a list has any duplicates, and if it does, it removes them.

Solution

Maybe your first idea is to iterate through the list. You compare every item with the other ones. If a duplicate is detected, then it is removed. Or maybe you traverse the list and store the first occurrence of the item in a new collection and ignore all the next occurrences of that item. Those are a typical approach, but sometimes what the interviewer expects is that you reuse the libraries included in the JDK.

We use *Set* from the Collections library. By definition, *Set* does not allow duplicates. Then, use the *sort* method to order it.

A Comparable interface sorts lists of custom objects in natural ordering. List of Objects that already implement Comparable (e.g., String) can be sorted automatically by Collections.sort.

LinkedHashSet (Collection list) is used to initialize a HashSet with the items of the list, removing the duplicates. Listing 14.1 shows this implementation.

Listing 14.1 - Remove duplicates from a list.

```java
public class ListUtils {
  public static <E extends Comparable<E>>
    List<E> removeDuplicatesAndOrder(List<E> list) {
    Set<E> set = new LinkedHashSet<>(list);
    ArrayList<E> arrayList = new ArrayList<>(set);
    Collections.sort(arrayList);
    return arrayList;
  }
}
```

Tests

```java
@Test
public void givenStringsThenRemovedDuplicates() {
  List<String> input = new ArrayList<>();
```

```java
    input.add("c");
    input.add("b");
    input.add("b");
    input.add("d");
    input.add("c");
    input.add("a");
    List<String> result = ListUtils.removeDuplicatesAndOrder(input);
    assertEquals("[a, b, c, d]", result.toString());
}

@Test
public void givenIntegersThenRemovedDuplicates() {
    List<Integer> input = new ArrayList<>();
    input.add(Integer.valueOf(3));
    input.add(Integer.valueOf(3));
    input.add(Integer.valueOf(4));
    input.add(Integer.valueOf(1));
    input.add(Integer.valueOf(7));
    input.add(Integer.valueOf(1));
    input.add(Integer.valueOf(2));
    input.add(Integer.valueOf(1));
    List<Integer> result = ListUtils.removeDuplicatesAndOrder(input);
    assertEquals("[1, 2, 3, 4, 7]", result.toString());
}
```

15. Given an integer N, returns its Factorial

The **factorial** is the **product** of all positive integers less than or equal to the non-negative integer. In real life, the factorial is the number of ways you can arrange *n* objects.

Solution

We make use of recursion. A recursive function is one that is defined in terms of itself. We always include a base case to finish the recursive calls.

Each time a function calls itself, its arguments are stored on the stack before the new arguments take effect. Each call creates *new local variables*. Thus, each call has its copy of arguments and local variables. That is one reason that we don't need to use recursion in the Production environment when we pass a big integer, they can overflow the stack and crash any application. Time complexity is O(N). Listing 15.1 shows the algorithm.

```
factorial(6)
= 6 * factorial(5)
= 6 * 5 * factorial(4)
= 6 * 5 * 4 * factorial(3)
= 6 * 5 * 4 * 3 * factorial(2)
= 6 * 5 * 4 * 3 * 2 * factorial(1)    ← base case
= 6 * 5 * 4 * 3 * 2 * 1
= 6 * 5 * 4 * 3 * 2
= 6 * 5 * 4 * 6
= 6 * 5 * 24
= 6 * 120
= 720
```

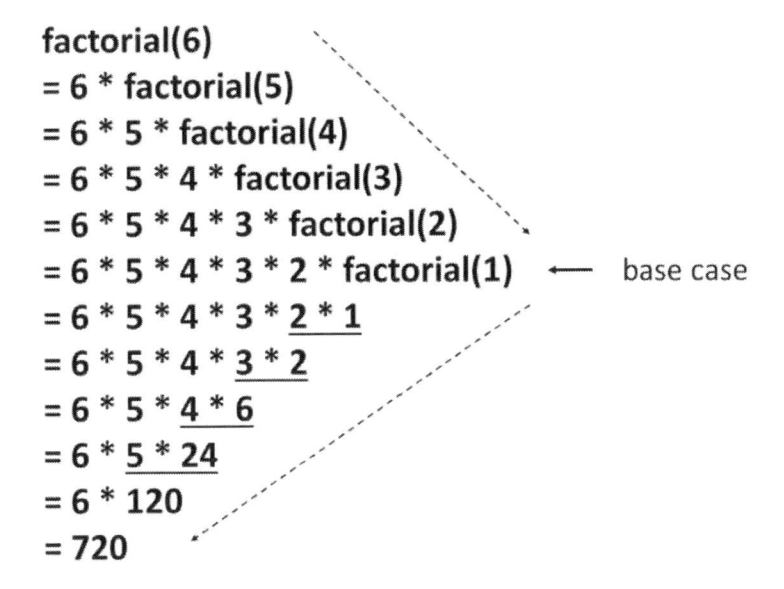

Figure 15.1 N Factorial

Listing 15.1 – Given an integer N, returns its Factorial

```java
public class FactorialRecursive {
  public static int factorial(int N) {
    if (N <= 1) //base case
      return 1;
    else
      return (N * factorial(N - 1));
  }
}
```

Listing 15.2 shows the iterative version (and more efficient).

Listing 15.2 – Given an integer N, returns its Factorial

```java
public class FactorialIterative {
  public static int factorial(int N) {
    int result = 1;
    for (int i=2; i<=N; i++)
      result*=i;
    return result;
  }
}
```

Tests

```java
public class FactorialRecursiveTest {

  @Test
  public void test_right_results() {
    assertTrue(FactorialRecursive.factorial(1) == 1);
    assertTrue(FactorialRecursive.factorial(0) == 1);
    assertTrue(FactorialRecursive.factorial(3) == 6);
    assertTrue(FactorialRecursive.factorial(6) == 720);
  }

  @Test
  public void test_wrong_results() {
    assertFalse(FactorialRecursive.factorial(3) == 5);
    assertFalse(FactorialRecursive.factorial(4) == 10);
  }
}
```

16. Bubble Sort

Bubble Sort uses a not sorted array, which contains at least two adjacent elements that are out of order. The algorithm repeatedly passes through the array, swapping elements that are out of order, and continues until it cannot find any more swaps.

Solution

The algorithm uses a Boolean variable to keep track of whether it has found a swap in its most recent pass through the array; as long as the variable is True, the algorithm loops through the Array, looking for adjacent pairs of elements that are out of order and swap them. The time complexity, in the worst case it requires $O(n^2)$ comparisons. Listing 16.1 shows the algorithm.

Listing 16.1 - Bubble Sort

```java
public class Sorting {

  public int[] bubbleSort(int[] numbers) {
    if (numbers == null)
      return numbers;

    boolean numbersSwapped;
    do {
      numbersSwapped = false;
      for (int i = 0; i < numbers.length - 1; i++) {
        if (numbers[i] > numbers[i + 1]) {
          int aux = numbers[i + 1];
          numbers[i + 1] = numbers[i];
          numbers[i] = aux;
          numbersSwapped = true;
        }
      }
    } while (numbersSwapped);

    return numbers;
  }
}
```

Example:
First pass-through:
{**6**, **4**, 9, 5} -> {**4**, **6**, 9, 5} swap because of 6 > 4
{4, **6**, **9**, 5} -> {4, **6**, **9**, 5}
{4, 6, **9**, **5**} -> {4, 6, **5**, **9**} swap because of 9 > 5

NumbersSwapped=true

Second pass-through:
{**4, 6**, 5, 9} -> {**4, 6**, 5, 9}
{4, **6, 5**, 9} -> {4, **5, 6**, 9} swap because of 6 > 5
{4, 5, **6, 9**} -> {4, 5, **6, 9**}
NumbersSwapped=true

Third pass-through:
{**4, 5**, 6, 9} -> {**4, 5**, 6, 9}
{4, **5, 6**, 9} -> {4, **5, 6**, 9}
{4, 5, **6, 9**} -> {4, 5, **6, 9**}
NumbersSwapped=false

The Efficiency of Bubble Sort

In a worst-case scenario, where the array comes in descending order, we need a swap for each comparison. In our algorithm, a comparison happens when we compare for adjacent pairs of elements to determine which one is greater.

Given an array: {9, 6, 5, 4}

In the first pass through, we have to make three comparisons -> {6, 5, 4, 9}

In our second passthrough, we have to make only two comparisons, because we didn't need to compare the final two numbers -> {5, 4, 6, 9}

In our third pass through, we made just one comparison -> {4, 5, 6, 9}

In summarize:
3 + 2 + 1 = 6 comparisons, or (N-1) + (N-2) + (N-3) ... + 1 comparisons

Moreover, in this scenario, we need a swap for each comparison. Therefore, we have six comparisons and six swaps = 12, which is approximately 4^2. As the number of items N increase, exponentially grows the number of steps as we can see in table 16.1

Therefore, in Big O Notation, we could say that the Bubble Sort algorithm has an efficiency of $O(N^2)$.

N	# steps	N^2
4	12	16
5	20	25
10	90	100

Table 16.1 Bubble sort efficiency

Tests

```java
public class BubbleSortTest {

    private Sorting sorting;

    @Before
    public void Before() {
        sorting = new Sorting();
    }

    @Test
    public void sortingArrays() {
        final int[] numbers = {6, 4, 9, 5};
        final int[] expected = {4, 5, 6, 9};
        int[] numbersSorted = sorting.bubbleSort(numbers);
        assertArrayEquals(expected, numbersSorted);
    }

    @Test
    public void sortManyElementArray() {
        final int[] array = {7, 9, 1, 4, 9, 12, 4, 13, 9};
        final int[] expected = {1, 4, 4, 7, 9, 9, 9, 12, 13};
        sorting.bubbleSort(array);
        assertArrayEquals(expected, array);
    }
}
```

17. Insertion Sort

Insertion sort is a sorting algorithm that builds the final sorted array one element at a time. It's similar to the way we sort playing cards in our hands.

Solution

Iterates over all the elements and start at index i=1.
Compare the current element (key) with all its preceding elements.
If the key element is smaller than its predecessors, swap them. Move elements that are greater than the key, one position ahead of their current position.

This algorithm takes a quadratic running time $O(n^2)$. Listing 17.1 shows the algorithm.

Listing 17.1 - Insertion Sort

```java
public class Sorting {

  public int[] insertSort(int[] numbers) {
    if (numbers == null)
      return numbers;

    for (int i=1; i<numbers.length; i++) {
      int key = numbers[i];
      int j = i-1;
      while (j>=0 && numbers[j]>key) {
        numbers[j+1] = numbers[j];
        j = j-1;
      }
      numbers[j+1] = key;
    }

    return numbers;
  }
}
```

Example:
numbers = {13, 12, 14, 6, 7}

When i = 1. Since 13 is greater than 12, move 13 and insert 12 before 13
12, 13, 14, 6, 7

When i = 2., 14 will remain at its position as all previous elements are smaller than 14
12, 13, 14, 6, 7

When i = 3., 6 will move to the beginning, and all other elements from 12 to 14 will move one position ahead of their current position.
6, 12, 13, 14, 7

When i = 4., 7 will move to the position after 6, and elements from 12 to 14 will move one position ahead of their current position.
6, 7, 12, 13, 14

Tests

```java
public class InsertSortTest {

    private Sorting sorting;

    @Before
    public void Before() {
        sorting = new Sorting();
    }

    @Test
    public void test_insertionSort() {
        final int[] numbers = {13, 12, 14, 6, 7};
        final int[] expected = {6, 7, 12, 13, 14};
        sorting.insertSort(numbers);
        assertArrayEquals(expected, numbers);
    }

    @Test
    public void sortingArray() {
        final int[] numbers = {7, 9, 1, 4, 9, 12, 4, 13, -2, 9};
        final int[] expected = {-2, 1, 4, 4, 7, 9, 9, 9, 12, 13};
        sorting.insertSort(numbers);
        assertArrayEquals(expected, numbers);
    }
}
```

18. Quick Sort

QuickSort is a divide and conquer algorithm. Given an array, it picks an element as pivot and partitions the given array around the chosen pivot.

Solution

Given an array, we execute the following **in-place** steps:

1. We pick from the array, the last element as our pivot.
2. We execute a partition operation, where we put all smaller elements before the pivot and put all greater elements after the pivot. After this reorder of elements, the pivot is in its final and correct position.
3. Apply the above steps recursively to every sub-array of elements.

Listing 18.1 shows the algorithm.

Listing 18.1 - Quick Sort

```java
public class Sorting {

  public int[] quickSort(int[] numbers, int lo, int hi) {
    if (lo < hi) {
      int partition_border =partition(numbers, lo, hi);
      //sort elements recursively
      quickSort(numbers, lo, partition_border-1);
      quickSort(numbers, partition_border+1, hi);
    }
    return numbers;
  }

  private int partition(int[] numbers, int lo, int hi) {
    //element to be placed at right position
    int pivot = numbers[hi];
    int i = lo -1; //index of smaller element
    for (int j = lo; j < hi; j++) {
      //swap when element smaller than the pivot
      if (numbers[j] < pivot) {
        i++;
        int aux = numbers[i];
        numbers[i] = numbers[j];
        numbers[j] = aux;
      }
    }
```

```java
      numbers[hi] = numbers[i+1];
      numbers[i+1] = pivot;
      return i+1;
   }
}
```

Tests

```java
public class QuickSortTest {

   private Sorting sorting;

   @Before
   public void Before() {
      sorting = new Sorting();
   }

   @Test
   public void test_quickSort() {
      final int[] numbers = {13, 12, 14, 6, 7};
      final int[] expected = {6, 7, 12, 13, 14};
      sorting.quickSort(numbers, 0, numbers.length-1);
      assertArrayEquals(expected, numbers);
   }

   @Test
   public void sortingArray() {
      final int[] numbers = {7, 9, 1, 4, 9, 12, 4, 13, -2, 9};
      final int[] expected = {-2, 1, 4, 4, 7, 9, 9, 9, 12, 13};
      sorting.quickSort(numbers, 0, numbers.length-1);
      assertArrayEquals(expected, numbers);
   }
}
```

19. Binary Search

Given a sorted array of N elements, write a function to search a given element X in the Array.

Solution

Search the sorted array by repeatedly dividing the search interval in half. If the element X is less than the item in the middle of the interval, narrow the interval to the lower half. Otherwise, narrow it to the upper half. Repeatedly check until the value is found or the interval is empty. Figure 19.1 shows the iteration when we search for 21. Time complexity is O (log n). If we pass an array of 4 billion elements, it takes at most 32 comparisons. Listing 19.1 shows the algorithm.

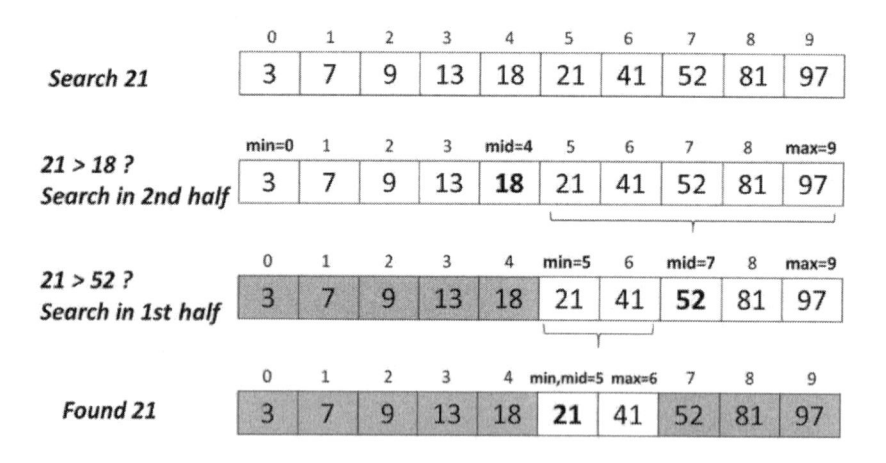

Figure 19.1 Binary Search example

Listing 19.1 Binary Search

```
public class BinarySearch {

  public static <T extends Comparable<T>>
    boolean search(T target, T[] array) {

    if (array == null || array.length <= 0)
```

```java
      return false;

    int min = 0;
    int max = array.length - 1;
    while (min <= max) {
      int mid = (min + max) / 2;
      if (target.compareTo(array[mid]) < 0) {
        max = mid - 1;
      } else if (target.compareTo(array[mid]) > 0) {
        min = mid + 1;
      } else {
        return true;
      }
    }
    return false;
  }
}
```

Tests

```java
public class BinarySeachTest {

  @Test
  public void binarySearch_target_notFound() {
    assertFalse(BinarySearch.search("fin",
        new String[]{"ada", "fda"}));
    assertFalse(BinarySearch.search("eda",
        new String[]{"ada", "bda", "cda", "dda"}));
  }

  @Test
  public void binarySearch_target_Found() {
    assertTrue(BinarySearch.search("cal",
      new String[]{"ada", "cal", "fda"}));
    assertTrue(BinarySearch.search(21,
      new Integer[]{3,7,9,13,18,21,41,52,81,97}));
  }
}
```

20. Rotate the matrix by 90 degrees

Given a square matrix, turn it by 90 degrees in a clockwise direction.

Solution

We build two for loops, an outer one deals with one layer of the matrix per iteration, and an inner one deals with the rotation of the elements of the layers. We rotate the elements in n/2 cycles. In every square cycle, we swap the elements with the corresponding cell in the matrix by using a temporary variable. Listing 20.1 shows the algorithm.

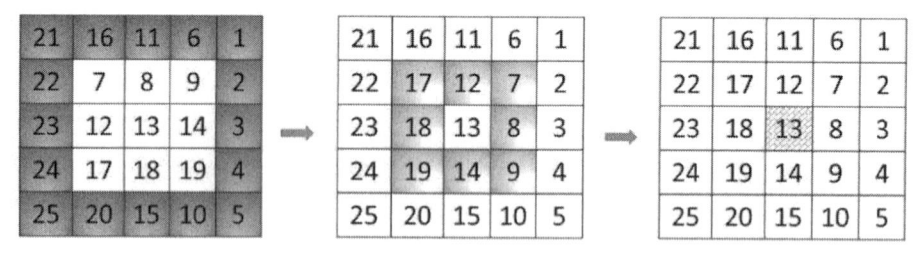

Figure 20.1 Rotate matrix by 90 degrees

Listing 20.1 – Rotate the Matrix by 90 degrees.

```java
public class MatrixUtils {
  public static void rotate(int[][] matrix) {
    int n = matrix.length;
    if (n <=1)
      return;

    /* layers */
    for (int i = 0; i < n / 2; i++) {
      /* elements */
      for (int j = i; j < n - i - 1; j++) {
        //Swap elements in the clockwise direction
```

```java
            //temp = top-left
            int temp = matrix[i][j];

            //top-left <- bottom-left
            matrix[i][j] = matrix[n - 1 - j][i];

            //bottom-left <- bottom-right
            matrix[n - 1 - j][i] = matrix[n - 1 - i][n - 1 - j];

            //bottom-right <- top-right
            matrix[n - 1 - i][n - 1 - j] = matrix[j][n - 1 - i];

            //top-right <- top-left
            matrix[j][n - 1 - i] = temp;
        }
    }
  }
}
```

Tests

```java
public class MatrixUtilsTest {

  @Test
  public void rotate4x4() {
    int[][] matrix = new int[][]{
        {9, 10, 11, 12},
        {16, 17, 18, 19},
        {23, 24, 25, 26},
        {30, 31, 32, 33}};
    MatrixUtils.rotate(matrix);
    assertArrayEquals(new int[]{30, 23, 16, 9}, matrix[0]);
    assertArrayEquals(new int[]{33, 26, 19, 12}, matrix[3]);
  }

  @Test
  public void rotate5x5() {
    int[][] matrix = new int[][]{
      {1, 2, 3, 4, 5},
      {6, 7, 8, 9, 10},
      {11, 12, 13, 14, 15},
      {16, 17, 18, 19, 20},
      {21, 22, 23, 24, 25}};
    MatrixUtils.rotate(matrix);
    assertArrayEquals(new int[]{21, 16, 11, 6, 1}, matrix[0]);
    assertArrayEquals(new int[]{22, 17, 12, 7, 2}, matrix[1]);
  }
}
```

21. Delimiter Matching

Check if the parentheses, braces, and brackets in an expression are balanced. In doing so, we must ensure that:

- Each opening symbol on the left delimiter matches a closing symbol on the right delimiter.
- Left delimiters that occur later should be closed before those occurring earlier.

Solution

We use a *stack* data structure to make sure two delimiting symbols match up correctly (right pair). Why stack? Because insertion and deletion of items take place at one end called top of the Stack. It's also named a LIFO (Last In, First Out). The JDK includes the `java.util.Stack` data structure. The *push* method adds an item to the top of this stack. The *pop* method removes the item at the top of this stack.

Iterate every character from the given expression. If it is an opening symbol, *push* that symbol onto the stack. If it is a closing symbol, *pop* an element from the stack (the last opening symbol added) and check that these symbols are a right pair. If we reach the end and the **stack is empty**, then the expression is balanced; otherwise, it is not balanced. Listing 21.1 shows the algorithm.

Listing 21.1 – Delimiter Matching

```
import java.util.Stack;
import java.util.function.Function;

public class IsDelimiterMatching implements Function<String, Boolean> {

  @Override
  public Boolean apply(String expression) {
    return isBalanced(expression);
  }

  private static boolean isBalanced(String expression) {
    final String openingDelimiters = new String("([{");
    final String closingDelimiters = new String(")]}");
    if (expression == null || expression.trim().length() < 2) {
      return false;
    }

    int len = expression.length();
    Stack<Character> stackBuffer = new Stack<>();
```

```java
    for (char c : expression.toCharArray()) {
      //an opening delimiter was found
      if (openingDelimiters.indexOf(c) != -1) {
        stackBuffer.push(c);
      //a closing delimiter was found
      } else if (closingDelimiters.indexOf(c) != -1) {
        if (stackBuffer.isEmpty())
          return false;
        //we assume that the matching closing delimiters
        //are at the same index
        if (closingDelimiters.indexOf(c) !=
            openingDelimiters.indexOf(stackBuffer.pop()))
          return false;
      }
    }
    //all opening delimiters matched? Then true
    return stackBuffer.isEmpty();
  }
}
```

Tests

```java
public class IsDelimiterMatchingTest {

  Function<String, Boolean> delimiterMatching = new
IsDelimiterMatching();

  @Test
  public void incorrect_expressions() {
    assertFalse(delimiterMatching.apply(null));
    assertFalse(delimiterMatching.apply(""));
    assertFalse(delimiterMatching.apply("("));
    assertFalse(delimiterMatching.apply("(()a]"));
  }

  @Test
  public void correct_expressions() {
    assertTrue(delimiterMatching.apply("()"));
    assertTrue(delimiterMatching.apply("([])"));
    assertTrue(delimiterMatching.apply("{{([])}}"));
    assertTrue(delimiterMatching.apply("{{a([b])}c}dd"));
    assertTrue(delimiterMatching.apply("(w*(x+y)/z-(p/(r-q)))"));
  }
}
```

22. Queue via Stacks

Build a queue data structure using only two internal stacks.

Stacks are based on the LIFO principle, i.e., the element *inserted* at *last* is the *first* element to come *out* of the list. **Queues** are based on the FIFO principle, i.e., the element *inserted* at *first* is the *first* element to come *out* of the list.

Solution

Stacks and Queues are abstract at their definition. That means, for example, in the case of Queues, that we can implement its behavior using two stacks.

Then we create two stacks of `java.util.Stack`, inbox, and outbox. The *add* method pushes new elements onto the inbox. And the *peek* method will do the following:

- If the outbox is empty, refill it by popping each element from the inbox and pushing it onto the outbox.
- Pop and return the top element from the outbox.

Listing 22.1 shows the algorithm.

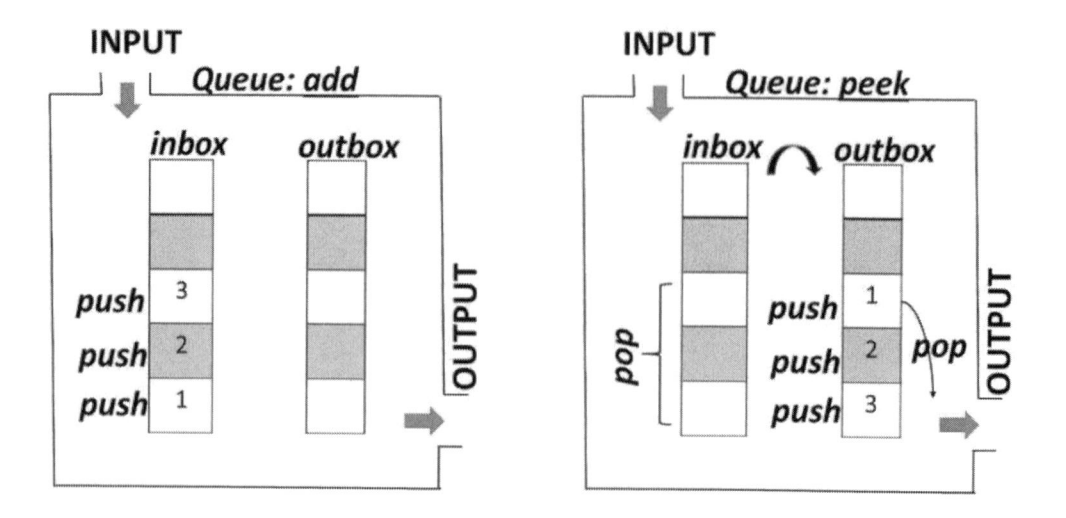

Figure 22.1 Queue via Stacks

Listing 22.1 – Queue via Stacks.

```java
public class QueueViaStacks<T> {
  Stack<T> inbox;
  Stack<T> outbox;

  public QueueViaStacks() {
    inbox = new Stack<>();
    outbox = new Stack<>();
  }

  public void add(T value) {
    //This stack always has the newest elements on top
    inbox.push(value);
  }

  public T peek() {
    if (outbox.isEmpty()) {
      while (!inbox.isEmpty()) {
        //Filled in inverse order
        outbox.push(inbox.pop());
      }
    }
    return outbox.pop();
  }
}
```

Tests

```java
public class QueueViaStacksTest {
  QueueViaStacks<Integer> queueViaStacks;

  @Before
  public void Before() {
    queueViaStacks = new QueueViaStacks<>();
  }

  @Test
  public void pop_firstElement() {
    queueViaStacks.add(4);
    queueViaStacks.add(2);
    queueViaStacks.add(9);
    assertEquals(new Integer(4), queueViaStacks.peek());
  }
}
```

23. Number of products of two consecutive integers

Given two integers X and Y, returns the number of integers from the range [X .. Y], which can be expressed as the product of two consecutive integers, e.g., N*(N+1) for some integer N.

Solution

We need to find the total number of products in this range [X .. Y].

Example:
Given X=6 and Y=20
The function should return 3

These integers are **6**=2*3, **12**=3*4, and **20**=4*5.

We could iterate from 1 until the upper limit=Y, checking if N*(N+1) <=Y. But if the lower limit is 1000, the first small products with two consecutive integers such as 1*2, 2*3, 3*4, does not fit in the range [1000, 1130], for instance. It is much better if we start the iteration from the square root of the lower limit X. Listing 23.1 shows the algorithm.

Listing 23.1 - Number of products of two consecutive integers.

```java
public class NumberUtils {
  public static int validProducts(int X, int Y) {
    if (X < 1)
      throw new IllegalArgumentException("invalid input: " + X);

    int N = (int)Math.sqrt(Integer.valueOf(X).doubleValue());
    int numberOfValidProducts = 0;
    while (N * (N + 1) <= Y) {
      int product = N * (N + 1);
      if (product >= X && product <= Y) {
        numberOfValidProducts++;
      }
      N++;
    }
    return numberOfValidProducts;
  }
}
```

Tests

```
@Test
public void test_right_products() {
  assertTrue(NumberUtils.validProducts(6, 20) == 3);
  assertTrue(NumberUtils.validProducts(1000, 1130) == 2);
}

@Test
public void test_wrong_products() {
  assertFalse(NumberUtils.validProducts(21, 29) == 1);
}
```

24. Return the most frequent elements of an array

Given an array, find the most frequent element in it.

Solution

Firstly, create a hash table.

Secondly, iterate the array and store elements and their frequency as key-value pairs. Then, traverse the hash table and inverse the order with the maximum frequency on top.

Finally, traverse the previous hash table, and build a list of the elements with maximum frequencies. Listing 24.1 shows the algorithm.

Listing 24.1 - Return the most frequent elements of an array.

```
import static java.util.stream.Collectors.*;

public class ArrayUtils {

  public static int[] mostFrecuent(int[] array) {

    Map<Integer, Integer> mapFrecuencyByElement = new HashMap<>();
    for (int element : array) {
      Integer frecuency = mapFrecuencyByElement.get(element);
      mapFrecuencyByElement.put(element, frecuency == null
      ? 1 : frecuency + 1);
    }

    Map<Integer, Integer> mapOrderedByTopFrecuency =
      mapFrecuencyByElement
        .entrySet()
        .stream()
        .sorted(Collections.reverseOrder(Map.Entry.comparingByValue()))
        .collect(
            toMap(Map.Entry::getKey, Map.Entry::getValue,
            (e1, e2) -> e2, LinkedHashMap::new)
        );

    List<Integer> result = new ArrayList<>();
```

```java
      int idx = 0; //to iterate the result list
      for (Map.Entry<Integer, Integer> entry :
        mapOrderedByTopFrecuency.entrySet()) {
        if (idx > 0) {
          //continue if exists same frequencies
          if (entry.getValue().equals(result.get(idx - 1))) {
            result.add(entry.getKey());
          } else {
            break;
          }
        } else {
          result.add(entry.getKey());
        }
        idx++;
      }

      int[] mostFrecuent = result.stream().mapToInt(i -> i).toArray();
      return mostFrecuent;
    }
}
```

Tests

```java
@Test
public void test_right_values() {
  assertArrayEquals(new int[]{2, 3},
      ArrayUtils.mostFrecuent(new int[]{3, 2, 0, 3, 1, 2}));
  assertArrayEquals(new int[]{5},
      ArrayUtils.mostFrecuent(new int[]{3, 5, 0, 5, 5, 1, 2}));
  assertArrayEquals(new int[]{7},
      ArrayUtils.mostFrecuent(new int[]{7}));
}
```

25. Assemble Parts in minimum Time

Write a method to calculate the minimum possible time to put the N parts together and build the final product. The input consists of two arguments: *numOfParts*, an integer representing the number of the parts, and *parts*, a list of integers representing the size of the parts.

Example:
numOfParts=4
parts=[8,4,6,12]

Output: 58

Explanation:
Step1: Assemble the parts of size 4 and 6 (time required is **10**). Then, the size of the remaining parts after merging: [8,10,12].

Step 2: Assemble the parts of size 8 and 10 (time required is **18**). Then, the size of the remaining parts after merging: [18,12].

Step 3: Assemble the parts of size 18 and 12 (time required is **30**).
The total time required to assemble the parts is 10+18+30=58.

Solution

We order the parts, then calculates the time between the two consecutive parts of small sizes until we arrive in the last part. Listing 25.1 shows the algorithm.

Listing 25.1 - Assemble Parts in minimum Time.

```
public class AssembleParts {
  public static int minimumTime(int numOfParts, List<Integer> list) {
    int[] arrayOfSizes = list.stream().mapToInt(i -> i).toArray();
    Arrays.sort(arrayOfSizes);

    int accumulatedTime = 0;
    for (int idx = 0; idx < arrayOfSizes.length - 1; idx++) {
      accumulatedTime += (arrayOfSizes[idx] + arrayOfSizes[idx + 1]);
      //once assembled, we carry the current time to the next element
```

```java
        //so in the next iteration, the first of the following two parts
        //it will already include the total time required
        //to assemble the two previous parts
        arrayOfSizes[idx + 1] = arrayOfSizes[idx] + arrayOfSizes[idx + 1];
      }
      return accumulatedTime;
    }
  }
```

Tests

```java
@Test
public void test_right_values() {
  assertTrue(AssembleParts.minimumTime(4,
      new ArrayList<Integer>(Arrays.asList(8, 4, 6, 12))) == 58);
  assertTrue(AssembleParts.minimumTime(5,
      new ArrayList<Integer>(Arrays.asList(3, 7, 2, 10, 5))) == 59);
}

@Test
public void test_wrong_values() {
  assertFalse(AssembleParts.minimumTime(3,
      new ArrayList<Integer>(Arrays.asList(2, 4, 6))) == 12);
}
```

26. Binary Search Tree

Tree structures are non-linear data structures. They allow us to implement algorithms much faster than when using linear data structures. A binary tree can have at the most two children: a left node and a right node. Every node contains two elements: a key used to identify the data stored by the node, and a value that is the data collected in the node.

The most common type of binary tree is the Binary Search Tree, which has two main characteristics:

- The value of the left node must be lesser than the value of its parent.
- The value of the right node must be greater than or equal to the value of its parent.

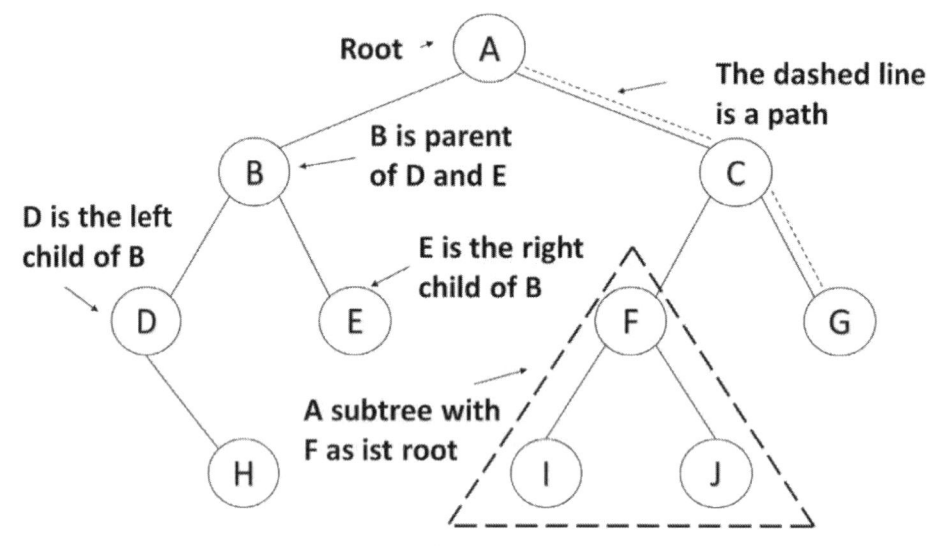

Figure 26.1 Binary Search Tree - terminology

You can search a tree quickly, as you can an ordered array, and you can also insert and delete items quickly, as you can with a linked list.

The Global Trade Item Number (GTIN) can be used by a company to identify all of its trade items uniquely. The GTIN identifies types of products that are produced by different manufacturers.

Use Case: A Webshop wants to retrieve information about GTINs efficiently by using a binary search algorithm.

Solution

Listing 26.1 shows how we create a Product Class.

Listing 26.1 - Product Class

```java
public class Product {
  Integer productId;
  String name;
  Double price;
  String manufacturerName;
  //setters and getters are omitted
}
```

Listing 26.2 shows how we create a NodeP Class to store a list of Products. Moreover, this Class allows us to have at the most two NodeP attributes to hold the left and right nodes.

Listing 26.2 - NodeP Class

```java
public class NodeP {

    private String gtin;
    private List<Product> data;
    private NodeP left;
    private NodeP right;

    public NodeP(String gtin, List<Product> data) {
        this.gtin = gtin;
        this.data = data;
    }
}
```

Listing 26.3 shows a TreeP Class to implement an abstract data type called binary search tree, which includes a NodeP root variable for the first element to be inserted. Then, every time a new GTIN is inserted, we need to implement an insert method, which compares the current GTIN versus the new GTIN. Depends on the result, we store the new GTIN on the left or the right Node. In this way, the insert method maintains an ordered binary search tree.

Listing 26.3 TreeP and insert method

```java
public class TreeP {

  private NodeP root;

  public void insert(String gtin, List<Product> data) {

    NodeP newNode = new NodeP(gtin, data);

    if (root == null)
      root = newNode;
    else {
      NodeP current = root;
      NodeP parent;
      while (true) {
        parent = current;
        if (gtin.compareTo(current.getGtin()) < 0) {
          current = current.getLeft();
          if (current == null) {
            parent.setLeft(newNode);
            return;
          }
        } else if (gtin.compareTo(current.getGtin()) > 0) {
          current = current.getRight();
          if (current == null) {
            parent.setRight(newNode);
            return;
          }
        } else
          return; //already exists
      }
    }
    return;
  }
}
```

Listing 26.4 shows a find method, which iterates through all nodes until a GTIN is found. With this algorithm, we reduce the search space to N/2 because the binary search tree is always ordered.

Listing 26.4 - find method

```java
public NodeP find(String gtin) {

  NodeP current = root;
```

```java
  if (current == null)
    return null;

  while (!current.getGtin().equals(gtin)) {
    if (gtin.compareTo(current.getGtin()) < 0) {
      current = current.getLeft();
    } else {
      current = current.getRight();
    }
    if (current == null) //not found in children
      return null;
  }
  return current;
}
```

Tests:

```java
@Test
public void test_findNode() {
    tree.insert("04000345706564",
      new ArrayList<>(Arrays.asList(product1)));
    tree.insert("07611400983416",
      new ArrayList<>(Arrays.asList(product2)));
    tree.insert("07611400989104",
      new ArrayList<>(Arrays.asList(product3, product4)));
    tree.insert("07611400989111",
      new ArrayList<>(Arrays.asList(product5)));
    tree.insert("07611400990292",
      new ArrayList<>(Arrays.asList(product6, product7, product8)));
    assertEquals(null, tree.find("07611400983324"));
    tree.insert("07611400983324",
      new ArrayList<>(Arrays.asList(product9)));
    assertTrue(tree.find("07611400983324") != null);
    assertEquals("07611400983324",
        tree.find("07611400983324").getGtin());
}
```

This Binary Search Tree works well when the data is inserted in random order. But when the values to be inserted are already ordered, a binary tree becomes unbalanced. With an unbalanced tree, we cannot find data quickly.

One approach to solving unbalanced trees is the red-black tree technique, which is a binary search tree with some unique features.

Assuming that we already have a balanced tree, listing 26.5 shows us how fast in terms of comparisons could be a binary search tree, which depends on a number N of elements. For instance, to find a product by GTIN in 1 billion products, the algorithm needs only 30 comparisons.

Listing 26.5 - Tree performance

```java
public class TreePerformance {
  public int comparisons(int N) {

    int acumElements = 0;
    int comparisons = 0;
    for (int level = 0; level <= N / 2; level++) {
      int power = (int) Math.pow(2, level);
      acumElements += power;
      if (acumElements >= N) {
        comparisons = ++level;
        break;
      }
    }
    System.out.println("comparisons -> " + comparisons);
    return comparisons;
  }
}
```

Tests:

```java
@Test
public void whenNelements_return_NroComparisons(){
  assertTrue(treePerformance.comparisons(15) <= 4);
  assertTrue(treePerformance.comparisons(31) <= 5);
  assertTrue(treePerformance.comparisons(1000) <=10);
  assertTrue(treePerformance.comparisons(1000000000) <=30);
}
```

27. Depth-First Search (DFS)

Implement the depth-first search algorithm to traverse a graph data structure.

Solution

A **Graph** is a non-linear **data structure** consisting of nodes (vertices) and edges. Its shape depends on the physical or abstract problem we are trying to solve. For example, if nodes represent cities, the routes which connect cities may be defined by *no-directed* edges. But if nodes represent tasks to complete a project, then their edges must be *directed* to indicate which task must be completed before another.

Terminology

A Graph can model the *Hyperloop* transport to be installed in Germany.

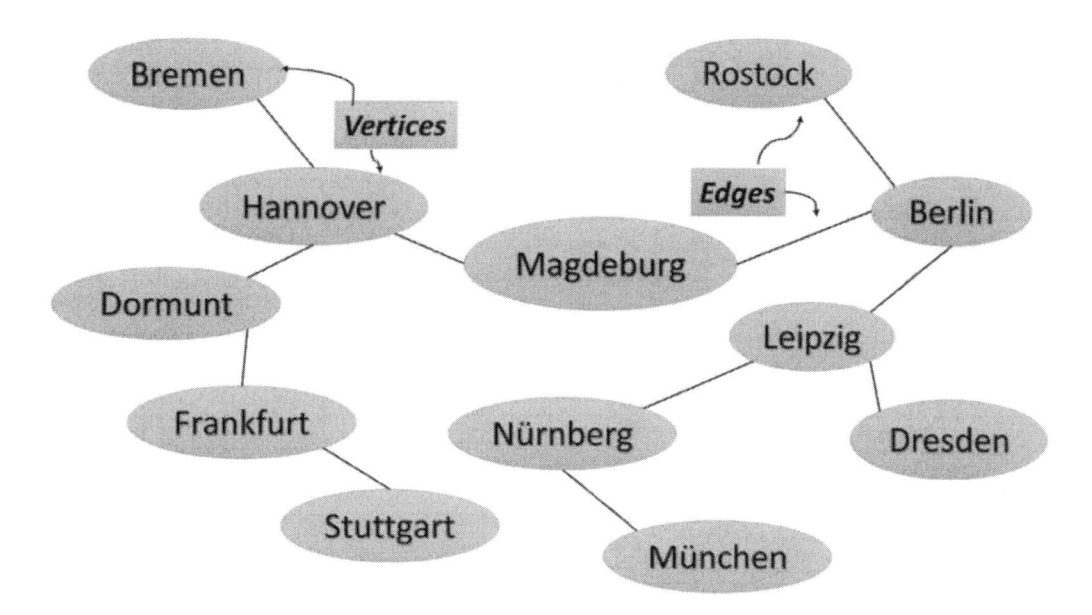

Figure 27.1 Graph - terminology

A Graph shows only the relationships between the *vertices* and the *edges*. The most important here is which edges are connected to which vertex. We can also say that Graph model connections between objects.

Adjacency

When a single edge connects two vertices, then they are adjacent or neighbors. In the figure above, the vertices represented by the cities, Berlin and Leipzig, are adjacent, but the cities Berlin and Dresden are not.

Path

A Path is a sequence of edges. The figure above shows a path from Berlin to München that passes through cities Leipzig and Nürnberg. Then the path is Berlin, Leipzig, Nürnberg, München.

Connected Graphs

A Graph is *connected* if there is at least one path from every vertex to every other vertex. The figure above is connected because all cities are connected.

Directed and Weighted Graphs

A Graph is directed when the edges have a *direction*. In the figure above, we have a non-directed graph because the **hyperloop** can usually go either way. From Berlin to Leipzig is the same as from Leipzig to Berlin.

Graphs are called a weighted graph when edges are given weight, e.g., the distance between two cities can be weighted in how fast they are connected.

One of the questions that a graph can answer is: which cities can be reached from a given City? We need to implement search algorithms. There are two different ways of searching in a graph: *depth-first search (DFS)* and *breadth-first search (BFS)*.

Depth-first search (DFS)

Depth-first search (DFS) is an algorithm for traversing the graph. The algorithm starts at the root node (selecting some arbitrary city as the root node) and explores as far as possible along each path. Figure 27.2 shows a sequence of steps if we choose Berlin as the root node.

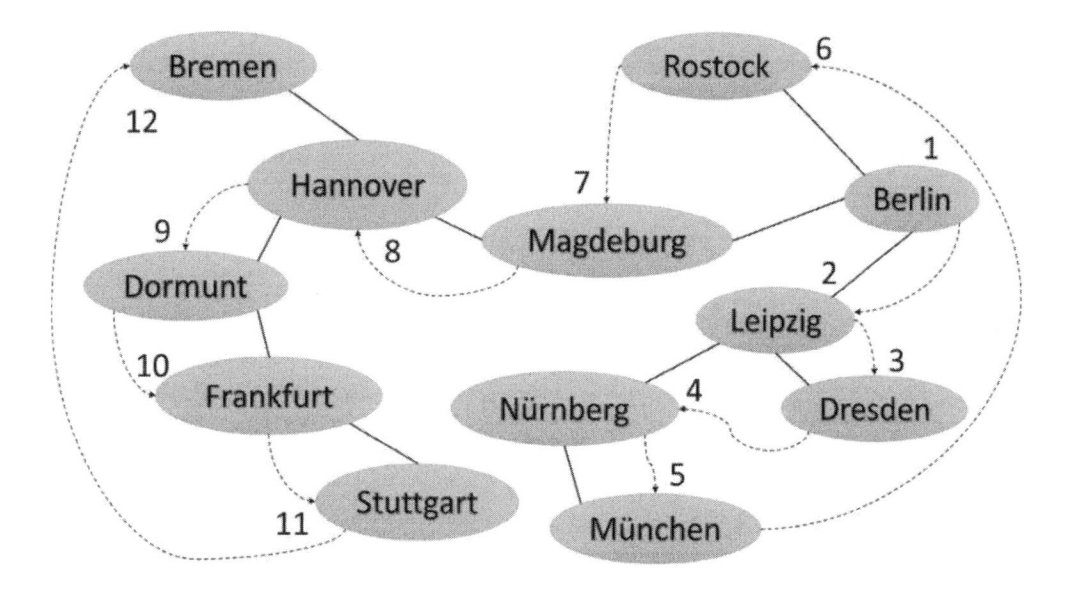

Figure 27.2 Depth-first search - the sequence of steps

Implementing the algorithm

Model the Problem

We need an Object which supports any kind of data included in the Node. We called it Vertex. We define a Boolean variable to avoid cycles in searching cities, so we will mark each node when we visit it. Listing 27.1 shows a Vertex Class implementation.

```
Listing 27.1 - Vertex Class


public class Vertex {
  private String name;
  private boolean visited;

  public Vertex(String name) {
    this.name = name;
    this.visited = false;
  }

  public String getName() {
    return name;
  }
  public void setName(String name) {
```

```
    this.name = name;
  }
  public boolean isVisited() {
    return visited;
  }
  public void setVisited(boolean visited) {
    this.visited = visited;
  }
}
```

Then, We will store these vertices in an array called *arrayOfVertex[]*.

To model how the vertices are connected (*edges*), we have two approaches: the *adjacency matrix* and the *adjacency list*. For this algorithm, we are going to implement the adjacency matrix.

The Adjacency Matrix

In a graph of N vertices, we create a two-dimensional array of NxN. An edge between two vertices (cities) indicates a connection (two adjacent nodes) and is represented by 1. No connections are represented by 0.

	Berlin	Leipzig	Dresden	Rostock	Nürnberg	...
Berlin	0	1	0	1	0	
Leipzig	1	0	1	0	1	
Dresden	0	1	0	0	0	
Rostock	1	0	0	0	0	
Nürnberg	0	1	0	0	0	

Table 27.1 Adjacency Matrix

The table 27.1 says, Leipzig is adjacent to Berlin, Dresden, and Nürnberg.

Create and Initialize an Abstract Data Type

We create an abstract data type called Graph to define the behavior of our data structure.

We need a *stack* so we can remember the visited vertices. When we add a new Vertex (City) and is stored in our *arrayOfVertex[]*, the *numOfVertices* variable indicates the number of Vertexes already added to the Graph.

Since we are going to pass a String argument to our DFS algorithm (city name), a *mapOfVertex* HashMap is defined to register the key-value: city-index. Listing 27.2 shows a Graph Class implementation.

```
Listing 27.2 Graph Class

public class Graph {

  private final int MAX_VERTEX = 15;
  private Vertex arrayOfVertex[]; //cities
  private Map<String, Integer> mapOfVertex;
  //matrix of adjacent vertex:
  private int matrixOfAdjVertex[][];
  //register the location at the arrayOfVertex:
  private int numOfVertices;
  private Stack<Integer> stack;

  public Graph() {
    arrayOfVertex =new Vertex[MAX_VERTEX];
    mapOfVertex =new ConcurrentHashMap<>();
    numOfVertices =0;
    matrixOfAdjVertex =new int[MAX_VERTEX][MAX_VERTEX];
    stack = new Stack<>();
    //initialize matrix
    for (int i=0; i<MAX_VERTEX; i++) {
      for (int j=0; j<MAX_VERTEX; j++) {
        matrixOfAdjVertex[i][j] =0;
      }
    }
  }
}
```

Adding a Vertex

```
public void addVertex(Vertex city) {
  mapOfVertex.put(city.getName(), numOfVertices);
```

```
    arrayOfVertex[numOfVertices++] =city;
}
```

The *numOfVertices* variable determines the location (index) of the new City in the *arrayOfVertex*[].

Adding an edge

We add two entries to *matrixOfAdjVertex*, because two cities are connected in both directions.

```
public void addEdge(String city1, String city2) {
  int start = mapOfVertex.get(city1);
  int end = mapOfVertex.get(city2);
  matrixOfAdjVertex[start][end] =1;
  matrixOfAdjVertex[end][start] =1;
}
```

The algorithm

Our *dfs()* method receives the City name as its argument. Then we locate the index of this city in our *HashMap*, and it is marked as visited and push it onto the stack.

We iterate the stack items *until it is empty*. And this is what we do in every iteration:

1. We retrieve the Vertex from the top of the stack (peek).
2. We try to retrieve at least one unvisited neighbor for this vertex.
3. If one vertex is found, it is marked as visited and pushes it onto the stack.
4. If one vertex is not found, we pop the stack.

If Berlin were our entry city, then the first adjacent city will be Leipzig, which is marked as visited and push it into the stack. In the next iteration, we read (peek) Leipzig from the stack and look for its neighbors. Through these iterations, we arrive at München. That is the *in-depth* essence of the algorithm. To explore as far as possible along each branch before continuing with a new one. Listing 27.3 shows the implementation of this algorithm.

```
Listing 27.3 Deep-First Search algorithm

public class Graph {

  //code omitted …
```

```java
  public void dfs(String city) {
    int vertex = mapOfVertex.get(city);
    arrayOfVertex[vertex].setVisited(true);
    System.out.print(city + " ");
    stack.push(vertex);

    while (!stack.isEmpty()) {
      int adjVertex = getAdjVertex(stack.peek());
      if (adjVertex != -1) {
        arrayOfVertex[adjVertex].setVisited(true);
        System.out.print(
            arrayOfVertex[adjVertex].getName() + " ");
        stack.push(adjVertex);
      } else {
        stack.pop();
      }
    }
  }

  //adjacent vertices not visited yet
  private int getAdjVertex(int vertex) {
    for (int adj=0; adj<numOfVertices; adj++) {
      if (matrixOfAdjVertex[vertex][adj] ==1 &&
          arrayOfVertex[adj].isVisited() ==false)
        return adj; //return first adjacent vertex
    }
    return -1; //not vertices found
  }

  public Map<String, Integer> getMapOfVertex() {
    return mapOfVertex;
  }

  public int[][] getMatrixOfAdjVertex() {
    return matrixOfAdjVertex;
  }
}
```

Tests

```java
public class GraphTest {

  Graph graph;

  @Before
  public void setup() {
    graph = new Graph();
  }
```

```java
@Test
public void test_addVertex() {
  Vertex city = new Vertex("Berlin");
  graph.addVertex(city);
  assertTrue(graph.getMapOfVertex().size() ==1);
}

@Test
public void test_addEdge() {
  String city1 ="Berlin";
  String city2 ="Leipzig";
  Vertex v1 = new Vertex(city1);
  Vertex v2 = new Vertex(city2);
  graph.addVertex(v1); //Location 0
  graph.addVertex(v2); //Location 1
  graph.addEdge(city1, city2);
  assertTrue(graph.getMatrixOfAdjVertex()[0][1] ==1);
  assertTrue(graph.getMatrixOfAdjVertex()[1][0] ==1);
}

@Test
public void test_dfs() {
  String city1 ="Berlin"; String city2 ="Leipzig";
  String city3 ="Dresden"; String city4 ="Nürnberg";
  String city5 ="Hannover"; String city6 ="Rostock";
  String city7 ="Dortmund"; String city8 ="Frankfurt";
  String city9 ="Stuttgart"; String city10 ="München";
  String city11 ="Magdeburg"; String city12 ="Bremen";
  graph.addVertex(new Vertex(city1));
  graph.addVertex(new Vertex(city2));
  graph.addVertex(new Vertex(city3));
  graph.addVertex(new Vertex(city4));
  graph.addVertex(new Vertex(city5));
  graph.addVertex(new Vertex(city6));
  graph.addVertex(new Vertex(city7));
  graph.addVertex(new Vertex(city8));
  graph.addVertex(new Vertex(city9));
  graph.addVertex(new Vertex(city10));
  graph.addVertex(new Vertex(city11));
  graph.addVertex(new Vertex(city12));
  graph.addEdge(city1, city2);
  graph.addEdge(city2, city3);
  graph.addEdge(city3, city4);
  graph.addEdge(city4, city10);
  graph.addEdge(city11, city5);
  graph.addEdge(city5, city7);
  graph.addEdge(city7, city8);
  graph.addEdge(city8, city9);
  graph.addEdge(city1, city6);
  graph.addEdge(city1, city11);
  graph.addEdge(city5, city12);
  graph.dfs(city1);
```

```
    }
}
```

Output:
Berlin Leipzig Dresden Nürnberg München Rostock Magdeburg Hannover Dortmund Frankfurt Stuttgart Bremen

We can change the entry city (Hannover) and see different traversing paths.

Output:
Hannover Dortmund Frankfurt Stuttgart Magdeburg Berlin Leipzig Dresden Nürnberg München Rostock Bremen

28. Breadth-First Search (BFS)

Implement the breadth-first search algorithm to traverse a graph data structure.

Solution

In the breadth-first search, the algorithm stays as close as possible to the starting point. It visits all the vertices adjacent to the starting vertex. The algorithm is implemented using a queue.

Figure 28.1 shows a sequence of steps if we choose Berlin as the root node. The numbers indicate the order in which the vertices are visited.

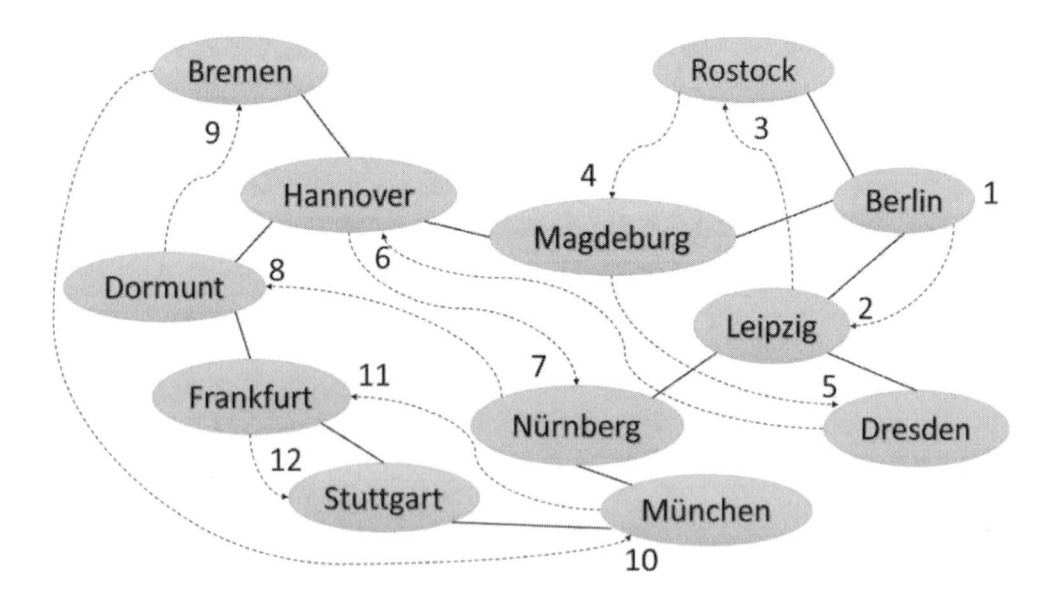

Figure 28.1 Breadth-First Search - the sequence of steps

The breath-first search algorithm first finds all the vertices that are one edge away from the starting vertex, then all the vertices that are two edges away, three edges away, and so on. It is useful to answer questions like what is the shortest path from Berlin to another city like München?

We traverse cities that are one edge away from Berlin (first level): Rostock, Magdeburg, and Leipzig. Then we traverse cities that are two edges away from Berlin (second level): Hannover, Nürnberg, and Dresden. Then we traverse cities that are three edges away from Berlin (third level): Bremen, Dortmund, and München. That's the idea. We already found

München before to traverse another possible path: Berlin, Magdeburg, Hannover, Dortmund, Frankfurt, Stuttgart, München, which corresponds to the sixth level.

Adding an edge

We use a LinkedList data structure to build our Adjacency List.
Two cities are adjacent or neighbors when a single edge connects them. Listing 28.1 shows the addEdge method.

Listing 28.1 - LinkedList, addEdge method

```java
private LinkedList<Integer> adjList[];


public void addEdge(String city1, String city2) {
  int start =mapOfVertex.get(city1);
  int end =mapOfVertex.get(city2);
  adjList[start].add(end);
  adjList[end].add(start);
}
```

The algorithm

Our *bfs()* method receives the City name as its argument. Then we locate the index of this city in our *HashMap*, and it is marked as visited, and add it onto the queue.

We iterate the queue items *until it is empty*. And this is what we do in every iteration:

1. We retrieve and remove the head Vertex of this queue (remove).
2. We iterate in an inner loop through all neighbors (adjacent) of this head Vertex until all they were visited. Every adjacent vertex is marked as visited and added to the queue.
3. When the previous iteration cannot find more adjacent vertices, then we retrieve and remove the new head Vertex.

Listing 28.2 - Breath-first search algorithm

```java
import java.util.*;
import java.util.concurrent.ConcurrentHashMap;

public class Graph {

  private final int MAX_VERTEX;
```

```java
  private Vertex arrayOfVertex[]; //cities
  private Map<String, Integer> mapOfVertex;
  //Adjacency list:
  private LinkedList<Integer> adjList[];
  //register the location at the arrayOfVertex:
  private int numOfVertices;
  private Queue<Integer> queue;

  public Graph(int vertices) {
    MAX_VERTEX =vertices;
    arrayOfVertex =new Vertex[MAX_VERTEX];
    mapOfVertex =new ConcurrentHashMap<>();
    numOfVertices =0;
    queue =new LinkedList<>();

    adjList =new LinkedList[MAX_VERTEX];
    for (int i =0; i<MAX_VERTEX; i++) {
      adjList[i] = new LinkedList();
    }
  }

  public void addVertex(Vertex city) {
    mapOfVertex.put(city.getName(), numOfVertices);
    arrayOfVertex[numOfVertices++] =city;
  }

  public void addEdge(String city1, String city2) {
    int start =mapOfVertex.get(city1);
    int end =mapOfVertex.get(city2);
    adjList[start].add(end);
    adjList[end].add(start);
  }

  public void bfs(String city) {
    int vertex =mapOfVertex.get(city);
    arrayOfVertex[vertex].setVisited(true);
    System.out.print(city + " ");
    queue.add(vertex);

    //iterate until queue empty
    while (!queue.isEmpty()) {
      int headVertex =queue.remove();
      int adjVertex;
      //iterate until it has no unvisited cities
      while ((adjVertex =getAdjVertex(headVertex)) != -1) {
        arrayOfVertex[adjVertex].setVisited(true);
        System.out.print(arrayOfVertex[adjVertex].getName() + " ");
        queue.add(adjVertex);
      }
    }
  }
```

```java
    //adjacent vertices not visited yet
    private int getAdjVertex(int vertex) {
      LinkedList linkedList = adjList[vertex];
      for (int adj=0; adj<linkedList.size(); adj++) {
        if (arrayOfVertex[(int) linkedList.get(adj)].isVisited() == false)
          return (int) linkedList.get(adj); //return first adjacent vertex
      }
      return -1; //not vertices found
    }

    public Map<String, Integer> getMapOfVertex() {
      return mapOfVertex;
    }

    public LinkedList<Integer>[] getAdjList() {
      return adjList;
    }
}
```

Tests

```java
public class GraphTest {

  Graph graph;

  @Before
  public void setup() {
    graph = new Graph(15);
  }

  @Test
  public void test_addVertex() {
    Vertex city = new Vertex("Berlin");
    graph.addVertex(city);
    assertTrue(graph.getMapOfVertex().size() ==1);
  }

  @Test
  public void test_addEdge() {
    String city1 ="Berlin";
    String city2 ="Leipzig";
    Vertex v1 = new Vertex(city1);
    Vertex v2 = new Vertex(city2);
    graph.addVertex(v1); //Location 0
    graph.addVertex(v2); //Location 1
    graph.addEdge(city1, city2);
    assertTrue(graph.getAdjList()[0].get(0) == 1);
    assertTrue(graph.getAdjList()[1].get(0) == 0);
  }
```

```java
@Test
public void test_bfs() {
  String city1 ="Berlin"; String city2 ="Leipzig";
  String city3 ="Dresden"; String city4 ="Nürnberg";
  String city5 ="Hannover"; String city6 ="Rostock";
  String city7 ="Dortmund"; String city8 ="Frankfurt";
  String city9 ="Stuttgart"; String city10 ="München";
  String city11 ="Magdeburg"; String city12 ="Bremen";
  graph.addVertex(new Vertex(city1));
  graph.addVertex(new Vertex(city2));
  graph.addVertex(new Vertex(city3));
  graph.addVertex(new Vertex(city4));
  graph.addVertex(new Vertex(city5));
  graph.addVertex(new Vertex(city6));
  graph.addVertex(new Vertex(city7));
  graph.addVertex(new Vertex(city8));
  graph.addVertex(new Vertex(city9));
  graph.addVertex(new Vertex(city10));
  graph.addVertex(new Vertex(city11));
  graph.addVertex(new Vertex(city12));
  graph.addEdge(city1, city2);
  graph.addEdge(city2, city3);
  graph.addEdge(city3, city4);
  graph.addEdge(city4, city10);
  graph.addEdge(city11, city5);
  graph.addEdge(city5, city7);
  graph.addEdge(city7, city8);
  graph.addEdge(city8, city9);
  graph.addEdge(city1, city6);
  graph.addEdge(city1, city11);
  graph.addEdge(city5, city12);
  graph.addEdge(city9, city10);
  graph.bfs(city1);
  }
}
```

Output:
Berlin Leipzig Rostock Magdeburg Dresden Hannover Nürnberg Dortmund Bremen München Frankfurt Stuttgart

29. Optimize online purchases

Given a budget *B* and a 2-D array, which includes [product-id][price][value], write an algorithm to optimize a basket with the most valuable products whose costs are less or equal than *B*.

Solution

Imagine that we have a budget of 4 US$ and we want to buy the most valuable snacks from the table 29.1.

Id	Name	Price US$	Amount gr.	Amount x US$
1	Snack Funny Pencil	0,48	36	75g
2	Snackin Chicken Protein	0,89	10	11g
3	Snacks Waffle Pretzels	0,98	226	230g
4	Snacks Tahoe Pretzels	0,98	226	230g
5	Tako Chips Snack	1,29	60	47g
6	Shrimp Snacks	1,29	71	55g
7	Rasa Jagung Bakar	1,35	50	37g
8	Snack Balls	1,65	12	7g
9	Sabor Cheese Snacks	1,69	20	12g
10	Osem Bissli Falafel	4,86	70	14g

Table 29.1 List of snacks

But who decides if a product is more valuable than another one? Well, this depends on every business. It could be an estimation based on quantitative or qualitative analysis. For our solution, we choose a quantitative approach based on which product gives us *more grams per every dollar invested*.

To implement our algorithm, we use the Red-Green Refactor technique, which is the basis of test-drive-development (TDD). In every assumption, we will write a test and see if it fails. Then, we write the code that implements only that test and sees if it succeeded, then we can refactor the code to make it better. Then we continue with another assumption and repeat the previous steps until the algorithm is successfully implemented for all tests.

To generalize the concept of "the most valuable product," we assign a value to every product. Our algorithm receives two parameters: an array 2-D, which includes [product-id][price][value], and the budget.

Assumption #1 - Given an array of products ordered by value, return the most valuable products

We start defining a java test creating a new BasketOptimized class.

```
Listing 29.1 - BaskedOptimized Test Case


public class BasketOptimizedTest {
  BasketOptimized basketOptimized;

  @Before
  public void setup() {
    basketOptimized = new BasketOptimized();
  }

  @Test
  public void productsOrderedByValue () {

    double[][] myProducts = new double[][] {
        {1, 0.98, 230},
        {2, 0.98, 230},
        {3, 0.48, 75},
        {4, 1.29, 55},
        {5, 1.29, 47},
        {6, 4.86, 14},
        {7, 1.69, 12},
    };

    double[][] mostValueableProducts =
        basketOptimized.fill(myProducts, 4);
    assertEquals(590d,
        Arrays.stream(mostValueableProducts).
            mapToDouble(arr -> arr[2]).sum(),0);
  }
}
```

The first time, it should fail because the *fill* method doesn't exist. Then we need to create an easy implementation to pass the test: the sum of the values must be equal to 590 because this represents all selected products, which its prices sum less than or equal to 4.

Now, we proceed to implement the *fill* method.

Listing 29.2 - BaskedOptimized fill method implementation

```java
public class BasketOptimized {

  public double[][] fill(double[][] myProducts, double budget) {

    int len = myProducts.length;
    double[][] mostValueableProducts = new double[len][3];

    double sum = 0;
    for (int idx=0; idx < len; idx++) {
      sum = sum + myProducts[idx][1]; //price
      if (sum <= budget) {
        mostValueableProducts[idx][0] =
            myProducts[idx][0]; //id
        mostValueableProducts[idx][1] =
            myProducts[idx][1]; //price
        mostValueableProducts[idx][2] =
            myProducts[idx][2]; //value
      }
    }
    return mostValueableProducts;
  }
}
```

Assumption #2 - Given an array of products not ordered by value, return the most valuable products

In this case, we pass a not ordered array, so we can see that our new test will fail.

```java
@Test
public void productsNotOrderedByValue () {
  double[][] myProducts = new double[][]{
      {1, 0.98, 230},
      {2, 1.29, 47},
      {3, 1.69, 12},
      {4, 1.29, 55},
      {5, 0.98, 230},
      {6, 4.86, 14},
      {7, 0.48, 75}
  };

  double[][] mostValueableProducts
    = basketOptimized.fill(myProducts, 4);
  assertEquals(590d, Arrays.stream(mostValueableProducts)
    .mapToDouble(arr -> arr[2]).sum(), 0);
}
```

We realize that we need to order the array by value because we want the most valuable products, so it is time to refactor our algorithm. What we need to do is to sort our input array.

```java
public double[][] fillBeta(double[][] myProducts, double budget) {
  Arrays.sort(myProducts, Collections.reverseOrder(
      Comparator.comparingDouble(a -> a[2])));
  int len = myProducts.length;
  double[][] mostValueableProducts =  new double[len][3];
```

Then we can see that our two first test cases were successful.

Assumption #3 - Given an array of products, we need to obtain the most valuable products from all possible combinations of the products

Imagine the following scenario:

```
double[][] myProducts = new double[][] {
            {1, 0.98, 230},
            {2, 0.51, 30},
            {3, 0.49, 28},
            {4, 1.29, 55},
            {5, 0.98, 230},
            {6, 4.86, 14},
            {7, 0.48, 75},
    };

double[][] mostValueableProducts = basketOptimized
        .fill(myProducts, 4);
assertEquals(590d,
      Arrays.stream(mostValueableProducts)
        .mapToDouble(arr -> arr[2]).sum(),0);
```

The test is expecting a result of 590, which corresponds to the final price of 3,73US$ (0.98+0.98+0.48+1.29). Once the algorithm sort by value the input array, we have the following result:

```
[1.0, 0.98, 230.0]
[5.0, 0.98, 230.0]
[7.0, 0.48, 75.0]
[4.0, 1.29, 55.0]
[2.0, 0.51, 30.0]
[3.0, 0.49, 28.0]
[6.0, 4.86, 14.0]
```

But here we realize the exists another combination of products which give us the most valuable products: 230+230+75+30+28 = 593, which corresponds to the final price of

3,44US$. Then we need to refactor our code to calculate all combinations (subsets) and return the most valuable products under a budget of 4 US$.

The subsets can be represented by all the binary options from 0 to 7 (the array size).

Bitwise operators allow to us manipulate the bits within an integer. For example, the int value for 33 in binary is 00100001, where each position represents a power of two, starting with 2^0 at the rightmost bit.

Listing 29.3 shows how many iterations the algorithm needs to do to build subsets of 1,2,3,4,5,6 or 7 products.

int numIterations = (**int**) Math.*pow*(2, myProducts.**length**);

So, for seven products, we have 128 iterations. And for every iteration, we build an inner loop to decide which products to include in a subset of products.

Let see an example:

When **int** idx = 33

We need to build a subset with those products which pass the following criteria:

if ((idx & (**int**) Math.*pow*(2, idx2)) == 0) {

The following table shows the iteration in our inner loop:

binary-idx	idx2	Math.*pow*(2,idx2)	binary-pow(idx2)	binary-idx **AND** binary-pow(idx2)
00100001	0	1	0001	1
00100001	1	2	0010	0
00100001	2	4	0100	0
00100001	3	8	1000	0
00100001	4	16	00010000	0
00100001	5	32	00100000	1
00100001	6	64	01000000	0

That means that a new subset will include those products located at indexes 1, 2, 3, 4, and 6 from our array of products.

And we need to ask if we can afford us to buy these products under our limited budget.

if (subSet.**length** > 0 && sumPrice <= budget) {

The following figure shows the result of our current iteration:

- idx = 33
- subSet = {double[7][]@1561}
  Not showing null elements
  - 0 = {double[3]@1131}
    - 0 = 2.0
    - 1 = 0.51
    - 2 = 30.0
  - 1 = {double[3]@1612}
    - 0 = 3.0
    - 1 = 0.49
    - 2 = 28.0
  - 2 = {double[3]@1067}
    - 0 = 4.0
    - 1 = 1.29
    - 2 = 55.0
  - 3 = {double[3]@1292}
    - 0 = 5.0
    - 1 = 0.98
    - 2 = 230.0
  - 4 = {double[3]@1641}
    - 0 = 7.0
    - 1 = 0.48
    - 2 = 75.0

We build a HashMap to store all combinations and the sum of its values. Finally, we return the first element of the HashMap, ordered by value.

```
Listing 29.3 - BaskedOptimized implementation
```

```java
public class BasketOptimized {

  public double[][] fill(double[][] myProducts, double budget) {

    int len = myProducts.length;
    int numIterations = (int) Math.pow(2, myProducts.length);

    Map<double[][], Double> combinations = new HashMap<>();

    for (int idx = 0; idx < numIterations; idx++) {
      double[][] subSet = new double[len][];
      double sumPrice = 0;
      double sumValue = 0;
      int i = 0;
      for (int idx2 = 0; idx2 < len; idx2++) {
        if ((idx & (int) Math.pow(2, idx2)) == 0) {
          subSet[i++] = myProducts[idx2];
          sumPrice = sumPrice + myProducts[idx2][1];
          sumValue = sumValue + myProducts[idx2][2];
```

```java
        }
      }
      if (subSet.length > 0 && sumPrice <= budget) {
        //remove nulls
        subSet = Arrays.stream(subSet)
            .filter(s -> (s != null && s.length > 0))
            .toArray(double[][]::new);
        combinations.put(subSet, Double.valueOf(sumValue));
      }
    }

    LinkedHashMap<double[][], Double> reverseSortedMap
      = new LinkedHashMap<>();

    combinations.entrySet()
        .stream()
        .sorted(Map.Entry.comparingByValue(Comparator.reverseOrder()))
        .forEachOrdered(x -> reverseSortedMap.put(x.getKey(),
          x.getValue()));

    double[][] mostValueableProducts = reverseSortedMap
        .keySet().iterator().next();
    return mostValueableProducts;
  }
}
```

Tests

```java
public class BasketOptimizedTest {

  BasketOptimized basketOptimized;

  @Before
  public void setup() {
    basketOptimized = new BasketOptimized();
  }

  @Test
  public void given_productsOrderedByValue_return_mostValueables() {

    double[][] myProducts = new double[][]{
        {1, 0.98, 230},
        {2, 0.98, 230},
        {3, 0.48, 75},
        {4, 1.29, 55},
        {5, 1.29, 47},
        {6, 4.86, 14},
        {7, 1.69, 12}
    };
```

```java
    double[][] mostValueableProducts
      = basketOptimized.fill(myProducts, 4);
    assertEquals(590d,
        Arrays.stream(mostValueableProducts).mapToDouble(arr ->
        arr[2]).sum(), 0);
}

@Test
public void given_productsNotOrderedByValue_return_mostValuables() {

    double[][] myProducts = new double[][]{
        {1, 0.98, 230},
        {2, 1.29, 47},
        {3, 1.69, 12},
        {4, 1.29, 55},
        {5, 0.98, 230},
        {6, 4.86, 14},
        {7, 0.48, 75}
    };

    double[][] mostValueableProducts
      = basketOptimized.fill(myProducts, 4);
    assertEquals(590d,
        Arrays.stream(mostValueableProducts).mapToDouble(arr ->
        arr[2]).sum(), 0);
}

@Test
public void given_products_return_theMostValuables() {

    double[][] myProducts = new double[][]{
        {1, 0.98, 230},
        {2, 0.51, 30},
        {3, 0.49, 28},
        {4, 1.29, 55},
        {5, 0.98, 230},
        {6, 4.86, 14},
        {7, 0.48, 75}
    };

    double[][] mostValueableProducts
      = basketOptimized.fill(myProducts, 4);
    assertEquals(593d,
        Arrays.stream(mostValueableProducts).mapToDouble(arr ->
    arr[2]).sum(), 0);
}
}
```

30. Tic tac toe

Write a tic-tac-toe program where the size of the board should be configurable between 3x3 and 9x9. It should be for three players instead of two, and its symbols must be configurable. One of the players is an AI. All three players play all together against each other. The play starts in random. The input of the AI is automatic. The input from the console must be provided in format X, Y. After every move, the new status of the Board is printed. The winner is who completes a whole row, column, or diagonal.

General Rules: https://en.wikipedia.org/wiki/Tic-tac-toe

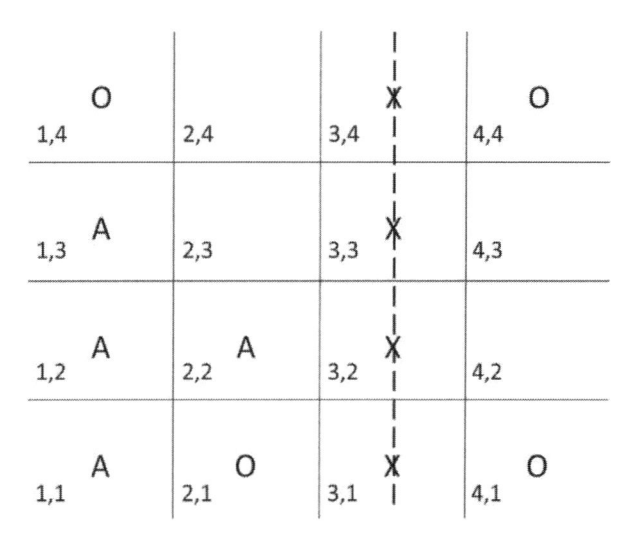

Figure 30.1 Tic-tac-toe game

Solution

What we learn from Object-Oriented Design and SOLID principles is that we need to delegate responsibilities to different components. For this game, we identify the following classes:

Board – set Size, get Winner, draw?
Player – (Human, IA)
Utils – to load configuration files.
App – the main class that assembly and control our different components.

Test case #1: Define the size of the Board

Based on the size of the Board, we need to initialize a bi-dimensional array to store the symbols after every move. Listing 30.1 shows one assumption about the setSize method.

```
Listing 30.1 - Board Class, setSize Test case
```

```java
public class BoardTest {

  private Board board;

  @Before
  public void setUp() {
    board = new Board();
  }

  @Test
  public void whenSizeThenSetupBoardSize() throws Exception {
    board.setSize(10);
    assertEquals(10, board.getBoard().length);
  }
}
```

Listing 30.2 shows an initial implementation of Board Class and the setSize method.

```
Listing 30.2 - Board Class, setSize method
```

```java
public class Board {

  private final static String EMPTY_ = " ";
  private String[][] board;

  public void setSize(int size) {
    this.board = new String[size][size];
    for (int x = 0; x < size; x++) {
      for (int y = 0; y < size; y++) {
        board[x][y] = EMPTY_;
      }
    }
  }
  public String[][] getBoard() {
    return board;
  }
}
```

TDD allows us to design, build, and test the smallest methods first and assemble them later. And the most important is that we can refactor it without breaking the rest of the test cases.

Test case #2: Enter a Symbol based on valid coordinates

Once the size is set up, we need to accept valid coordinates and check if that location is still available.

```java
@Test
public void whenCoordinatesAreNotBusyThenPutSymbol() throws Exception {
  board.setSize(3);
  board.putSymbol(1, 2, "X");
  board.putSymbol(2, 3, "O");
  assertEquals("O", board.getBoard()[1][2]);
}
```

Listing 30.3 shows the implementation of the putSymbol method.

```
Listing 30.3 - Board Class, putSymbol method
```

```java
public void putSymbol(int x, int y, String character) {
  if (x < 1 || x > this.board.length)
    throw new RuntimeException(
    "X coordinate invalid, must be between 1 and " +
    this.board.length);

  if (y < 1 || y > this.board.length)
    throw new RuntimeException(
    "Y coordinate invalid, must be between 1 and " +
    this.board.length);

  if (board[x - 1][y - 1] != EMPTY_)
    throw new RuntimeException("Coordinates are busy");

  board[x - 1][y - 1] = character;
}
```

If we set the size to 4, that means that for the player, the lower limit is 1, and the upper limit is 4.

Test case #3: After every move, print the Board

Every time a player enters valid coordinates, then the Board is updated and printed.

```java
@Test
public void whenBoardIsNotNullThenPrintIsPossible() {
  board.setSize(10);
```

```java
    board.putSymbol(1, 2, "X");
    board.putSymbol(2, 3, "O");
    board.print();
}
```

Listing 30.4 shows the implementation of the print method.

```
Listing 30.4 - Board Class, print method
```

```java
public void print() {
    if (board == null)
        throw new RuntimeException("Board is not initialized");

    int size = board.length;
    for (int y = size - 1; y >= 0; y--) {
        for (int x = 0; x < size; x++) {
            if (x == size - 1) {
                System.out.print(board[x][y] + "");
            } else {
                System.out.print(board[x][y] + "|");
            }
        }
        System.out.println("");
    }
}
```

Here you can even delegate the print of the Board to another component, e.g., Console.print. In this way, when you want to print in XML o HTML format, Console Class will be responsible for implementing the new methods. *There should never be more than one reason for a class to change.*

Test Case #4: Returns a winner

Once we set the size, the game receives different moves. The Board Class checks if in the game exists a winner after a move. Listing 30.5 defines a test case to check if a whole horizontal line is filled.

```
Listing 30.5 - Board Class, getWinner Test Case
```

```java
@Test
public void horizontalLineFilledThenWinnerX() {
    board.setSize(3);
    board.putSymbol(1, 1, "X");
    board.putSymbol(1, 2, "O");
    board.putSymbol(2, 1, "X");
```

```
  board.putSymbol(2, 3, "O");
  board.putSymbol(3, 1, "X");
  board.print();
  assertEquals("X", board.getWinner());
}
```

Then we iterate every horizontal line and check if it is filled with the same symbol. Listing 30.6 shows the implementation of the getWinner method.

Listing 30.6 - Board Class, getWinner method

```
public String getWinner() {

  if (board == null)
    throw new RuntimeException("Board is not initialized");

  String winner = null;
  for (int y = 0; y < board.length; y++) {
    String symbol = board[0][y];
    if (symbol != EMPTY_) {
      int counter = 1;
      for (int x = 1; x < board.length; x++) {
        if (symbol.equals(board[x][y])) {
          counter++;
        }
      }
      if (counter == board.length) {
        winner = symbol;
        return winner;
      }
    }
  }
  return winner;
}
```

We need the same logic for all the ways to win: vertical, diagonal, so we need to abstract every case in sub methods. Listing 30.7 shows the new getWinner method after refactoring.

Listing 30.7 - Board Class, getWinner method refactored

```
public String getWinner() {

  if (board == null)
    throw new RuntimeException("Board is not initialized");

  String winner = winnerInHorizonzalLine();
  if (winner != null) {
```

```
      return winner;
    } else {
      winner = winnerInVerticalLine();
      if (winner != null) {
        return winner;
      } else {
        winner = winnerInDiagonalBottomLeft();
        if (winner != null) {
          return winner;
        } else {
          winner = winnerInDiagonalTopLeft();
          if (winner != null) {
            return winner;
          } else {
            //we avoid iterating the whole board every time
            //to look for a draw
            if (this.numOfPlays == this.numOfPlaysAllowed) {
              return DRAW_;
            } else {
              return null;
            }
          }
        }
      }
    }
  }
}
```

The previous code show how we introduce three new variables:

A constant variable:

```
private final static String DRAW_ = "DRAW!";
```

`numOfPlays` and `numOfPlaysAllowed` are declared as member variables at the Board Class.

`numOfPlaysAllowed` is initialized at the setSize method:
```
this.numOfPlaysAllowed = size * size;
```

And the `numOfPlays` is incremented at the putSymbol method:

```
this.numOfPlays++;
```

```
private String winnerInVerticalLine() {
  String winner = null;
  for (int x = 0; x < board.length; x++) {
    String symbol = board[x][0];
```

```java
      if (symbol != EMPTY_) {
        int counter = 1;
        for (int y = 1; y < board.length; y++) {
          if (symbol.equals(board[x][y])) {
            counter++;
          }
        }
        if (counter == board.length) {
          winner = symbol;
          return winner;
        }
      }
    }
  }
  return winner;
}

private String winnerInDiagonalBottomLeft() {
  String winner = null;
  String symbol = board[0][0];
  if (symbol != EMPTY_) {
    int counter = 1;
    for (int idx = 1; idx < board.length; idx++) {
      if (symbol.equals(board[idx][idx])) {
        counter++;
      }
    }
    if (counter == board.length) {
      winner = symbol;
      return winner;
    }
  }
  return winner;
}

private String winnerInDiagonalTopLeft() {
  String winner = null;
  String symbol = board[0][board.length - 1];
  if (symbol != EMPTY_) {
    int counter = 1;
    for (int idx = 1; idx < board.length; idx++) {
      if (symbol.equals(board[idx][board.length - 1 - idx])) {
        counter++;
      }
    }
    if (counter == board.length) {
      winner = symbol;
      return winner;
    }
  }
  return winner;
}
```

Now let see the Utils Class, which load the symbols and the size of the Board.

Test case #5: Load file

We need a method that, given a Filename, retrieves the content of that File. Listing 30.8 shows the test case.

```
Listing 30.8 - Utils Test Class

public class UtilsTest {

   private Utils utils;

   @Before
   public void setUp() {
      utils = new Utils();
   }

   @Rule
   public ExpectedException thrownException = ExpectedException.none();

   @Test
   public void whenFileExistsThenReturnContent() throws Exception {
      String content = utils.loadFile("board.txt");
      assertNotNull(content);
   }
}
```

Assumes that our configuration files are located under the project name. Listing 30.9 shows a loadFile implementation.

```
Listing 30.9 - Utils Class, loadFile method

public class Utils {

   public String loadFile(String fileName) throws Exception {
      String content;
      try {
         content = new String(Files.readAllBytes(Paths.get(fileName)));
      } catch (IOException io) {
         throw new RuntimeException("File " + fileName + " not found");
      }
      return content;
   }
}
```

Test case #6: Get the Board size

Once a Board File is loaded, we need to validate includes a valid content. Listing 30.10 shows the assumption about how to validate the Board size. Based on the requirements, board size must be a value between 3 and 9.

```
Listing 30.10 - Utils Class, getBoardSize Test case

@Test
public void whenGetBoardSizeIs4ThenReturnSize() throws Exception {
  String content = utils.loadFile("board.txt");
  assertEquals(4, utils.getBoardSize(content));
}

board.txt
4
```

Listing 30.11 shows the implementation of the getBoardSize.

```
Listing 30.11 - Utils Class, getBoardSize method

public int getBoardSize(String content) throws Exception {

  if (content == null)
    throw new RuntimeException("Invalid setting for the board");

  if (Integer.valueOf(content) < 3 || Integer.valueOf(content) > 9)
    throw new RuntimeException("Invalid setting for the board");

  return Integer.valueOf(content).intValue();
}
```

Try always to build a small method for each thing. If you can divide the problem into small parts, that means that you can create great software in more significant projects

Test case #7: Get symbols

Once a symbol File is loaded, it validates that it is retrieved only three symbols. Listing 30.12 shows our assumption in the Test case.

```
Listing 30.12 - Utils Class, getSymbols Test Case

@Test
public void whenSymbolsIsThreeThenReturnValues() throws Exception {
  String content = utils.loadFile("symbols.txt");
```

```java
  String[] symbols = utils.getSymbols(content);
  assertArrayEquals(new String[]{"X","O","A"}, symbols);
}
```

```
symbols.txt
X,O,A
```

Listing 30.13 shows the getSymbols method implementation.

`Listing 30.13 - Utils Class, getSymbols method`

```java
public String[] getSymbols(String content) {
  String[] symbols = content.split(",");
  if (symbols.length != 3)
    throw new RuntimeException("Invalid settings for symbols");

  return symbols;
}
```

Test case #8: Receive input from the console

We create an auxiliary Input class to store the coordinates entered by the player. Listing 30.14 shows our assumption in a Test Case Class.

```java
public class Input {
  private int x;
  private int y;
}
```

`Listing 30.14 - Utils Class, getInput Test case`

```java
@Test
public void inputFromConsoleThenReturnInput() throws Exception {
  Input input = utils.getInputFromConsole("2,3");
  assertEquals(2, input.getX());
  assertEquals(3, input.getY());
}
```

Listing 30.15 shows the getInputFromConsole method implementation, where we need to accept valid numbers.

Listing 30.15 - Utils Class, `getInputFromConsole` method

```java
public Input getInputFromConsole(String inputFromConsole) {

  if (inputFromConsole == null || inputFromConsole.trim().length() <= 0)
    throw new RuntimeException("Invalid input from console");

  Pattern p = Pattern.compile("[0-9]*\\.?,[0-9]+");
  Matcher matcher = p.matcher(inputFromConsole);
  if (!matcher.find())
    throw new RuntimeException("Invalid input from console");

  String[] inputSplitted = inputFromConsole.split(",");

  Input input = new Input();
  input.setX(Integer.valueOf(inputSplitted[0]).intValue());
  input.setY(Integer.valueOf(inputSplitted[1]).intValue());
  return input;
}
```

Now, we implement the Player Class.

Listing 30.16 shows a design of a Player Class and its sub-classes.

Listing 30.16 - Player Class, and sub Classes

```java
public class Player {
  private String symbol;
  //getters and setters are omitted
}

public class Human extends Player {}

public class IA extends Player {}
```

Test case #9: Implements how IA plays

To make an easy tic tac toe program, we are going to allow that the IA player fills the first coordinate available on the board. Of course, you can write a more complex implementation based on graphs, for example, to decide the best move of the IA player. Listing 30.17 shows assumptions about the IA player.

Listing 30.17 - Player Class, **Test Cases**

```java
public class PlayerTest {

  private Player humanPlayer;
  private IA iaPlayer;
  private Board board;

  @Before
  public void setUp() {
    humanPlayer = new Human();
    iaPlayer = new IA();
    board = new Board();
    board.setSize(3);
  }

  @Test
  public void whenSetSymbolThenReturnSameSymbol() throws Exception {
    humanPlayer.setSymbol("A");
    assertEquals("A", humanPlayer.getSymbol());
  }

  @Test
  public void whenIAPlaysThenReturnInput() throws Exception {
    iaPlayer.setSymbol("A");
    board.putSymbol(1, 1, "X");
    board.putSymbol(2, 2, "O");
    board.print();
    Input input = iaPlayer.play(board.getBoard());
    assertEquals(1, input.getX());
    assertEquals(2, input.getY());
  }
}
```

Listing 30.18 shows the play method implementation.

Listing 30.18 - Player Class, **play method**

```java
public class IA extends Player {
  private final static String EMPTY_ = " ";

  public Input play(String[][] board) {
    Input input = new Input();
    //Assumption: find the first coordinate available
    for (int x = 0; x < board.length; x++) {
      for (int y = 0; y < board.length; y++) {
        String symbol = board[x][y];
        if (symbol.equals(EMPTY_)) {
          input.setX(x + 1);
```

```
              input.setY(y + 1);
              return input;
            }
          }
        }
      return input;
    }
}
```

Now that we have all components ready, it is time to build the main class. Listing 30.19 shows how App Class assembly all components.

```
Listing 30.19 - App Class

public class App {
  private final static String DRAW_ = "DRAW!";

  public static void main(String[] args) throws Exception {

    System.out.println("Welcome to TIC TAC TOE 2.0!");
    Scanner scanner = new Scanner(System.in);

    Utils utils = new Utils();
    int boardSize = utils.getBoardSize(utils.loadFile("board.txt"));

    Board board = new Board();
    board.setSize(boardSize);

    System.out.println("You are playing in a board " +
        boardSize + "x" + boardSize);
    String[] symbols =
        utils.getSymbols(utils.loadFile("symbols.txt"));

    Player player1 = new Human();
    player1.setSymbol(symbols[0]);
    Player player2 = new Human();
    player2.setSymbol(symbols[1]);
    Player player3 = new IA();
    player3.setSymbol(symbols[2]);

    List<Player> playersIterator = new ArrayList<>();
    playersIterator.add(player1);
    playersIterator.add(player2);
    playersIterator.add(player3);
    //made random
    Collections.shuffle(playersIterator);

    int idx = 0;
    boolean stillPlaying = true;
    while (stillPlaying) {
```

```java
      Player player = playersIterator.get(idx++);
      if (player instanceof IA) {
        System.out.println("Player " + player.getSymbol() +
          " enter your coordinates in Format x,y: ");
        Input input = ((IA) player).play(board.getBoard());
        board.putSymbol(input.getX(), input.getY(), player.getSymbol());
      } else {
        boolean coordinateOk = false;
        while (!coordinateOk) {
          System.out.println("Player " + player.getSymbol() +
            " enter your coordinates in Format x,y: ");
          try {
            Input input = utils.getInputFromConsole(scanner.nextLine());
            board.putSymbol(input.getX(),
              input.getY(), player.getSymbol());
            coordinateOk = true;
          } catch (RuntimeException ex) {
            System.out.println(ex.getMessage());
          }
        }
      }
      board.print();
      String winner = board.getWinner();
      if (winner != null) {
        stillPlaying = false;
        if (winner.equals(DRAW_)) {
          System.out.println(DRAW_);
        } else {
          System.out.println("Player " + winner + " is the Winner!");
        }
      }
      //to control the turn of every player
      if (idx == 3)
        idx = 0;
    }
  }
}
```

DEMO:
```
Welcome to TIC TAC TOE 2.0!
You are playing in a board 4x4
Player A enter your coordinates in Format x,y:
 | | |
 | | |
 | | |
A| | |
Player O enter your coordinates in Format x,y:
1,1
Coordinates are busy
```

Top Java Challenges

```
Player O enter your coordinates in Format x,y:
2,1
 | | |
 | | |
 | | |
A|O| |
Player X enter your coordinates in Format x,y:
3,4
 | |X|
 | | |
 | | |
A|O| |
Player A enter your coordinates in Format x,y:
 | |X|
 | | |
A| | |
A|O| |
Player O enter your coordinates in Format x,y:
    .
    .
    .
    .
O| |X|O
A| | |
A|A|X|
A|O|X|O
Player X enter your coordinates in Format x,y:
3,3
O| |X|O
A| |X|
A|A|X|
A|O|X|O
Player X is the Winner!
```

The next section includes all test cases:

Tests

```java
public class BoardTest {

    private Board board;

    @Before
    public void setUp() {
        board = new Board();
```

```java
}

@Rule
public ExpectedException thrownException = ExpectedException.none();

@Test
public void whenSizeThenSetupBoardSize() throws Exception {
  board.setSize(10);
  assertEquals(10, board.getBoard().length);
}

@Test
public void whenPutCharacterWrongCoordinateThenThrowError()
  throws Exception {
  board.setSize(4);
  thrownException.expect(RuntimeException.class);
  board.putSymbol(1, 5, "X");
}

@Test
public void whenCoordinateIsValidThenPutCharacterIsOk()
  throws Exception {
  board.setSize(3);
  board.putSymbol(1, 2, "X");
  assertEquals("X", board.getBoard()[0][1]);
}

@Test
public void whenCoordinatesAreBusyThenPutCharacterThrowError()
  throws Exception {
  board.setSize(3);
  board.putSymbol(1, 2, "X");
  thrownException.expect(RuntimeException.class);
  board.putSymbol(1, 2, "O");
}

@Test
public void whenCoordinatesAreNotBusyThenPutSymbol()
  throws Exception {
  board.setSize(3);
  board.putSymbol(1, 2, "X");
  board.putSymbol(2, 3, "O");
  assertEquals("O", board.getBoard()[1][2]);
}

@Test
public void whenBoardIsNullThenPrintThrowsError() {
  thrownException.expect(RuntimeException.class);
  board.print();
}
```

```java
@Test
public void whenBoardIsNotNullThenPrintIsPossible() {
  board.setSize(10);
  board.print();
}

@Test
public void horizontalLineIsNotSameSymbolThenReturnNull() {
  board.setSize(3);
  board.putSymbol(2, 2, "X");
  board.putSymbol(1, 2, "O");
  board.putSymbol(1, 3, "X");
  board.putSymbol(2, 1, "O");
  board.putSymbol(3, 2, "X");
  board.print();
  assertEquals(null, board.getWinner());
}

@Test
public void horizontalLineFilledThenWinnerX() {
  board.setSize(3);
  board.putSymbol(1, 1, "X");
  board.putSymbol(1, 2, "O");
  board.putSymbol(2, 1, "X");
  board.putSymbol(2, 3, "O");
  board.putSymbol(3, 1, "X");
  board.print();
  assertEquals("X", board.getWinner());
}

@Test
public void horizontalLineFilledThenWinnerO() {
  board.setSize(4);
  board.putSymbol(1, 1, "X");
  board.putSymbol(1, 4, "O");
  board.putSymbol(2, 1, "X");
  board.putSymbol(2, 4, "O");
  board.putSymbol(3, 1, "X");
  board.putSymbol(3, 4, "O");
  board.putSymbol(3, 3, "X");
  board.putSymbol(4, 4, "O");
  board.print();
  assertEquals("O", board.getWinner());
}

@Test
public void verticalLineIsSameSymbolThenReturnWinnerX() {
  board.setSize(3);
  board.putSymbol(2, 1, "X");
  board.putSymbol(1, 3, "O");
  board.putSymbol(2, 2, "X");
  board.putSymbol(3, 3, "O");
```

```java
    board.putSymbol(2, 3, "X");
    board.print();
    assertEquals("X", board.getWinner());
}

@Test
public void diagonalLineSameSymbolThenReturnWinnerX() {
    board.setSize(3);
    board.putSymbol(1, 1, "X");
    board.putSymbol(1, 2, "O");
    board.putSymbol(2, 2, "X");
    board.putSymbol(2, 1, "O");
    board.putSymbol(3, 3, "X");
    board.print();
    assertEquals("X", board.getWinner());
}

@Test
public void diagonalLineSameSymbolThenReturnWinnerO() {
    board.setSize(3);
    board.putSymbol(1, 1, "X");
    board.putSymbol(1, 3, "O");
    board.putSymbol(3, 2, "X");
    board.putSymbol(2, 2, "O");
    board.putSymbol(3, 3, "X");
    board.putSymbol(3, 1, "O");
    board.print();
    assertEquals("O", board.getWinner());
}

@Test
public void diagonalLineSameSymbolThenReturnWinnerX_2() {
    board.setSize(5);
    board.putSymbol(1, 1, "O");
    board.putSymbol(1, 5, "X");
    board.putSymbol(3, 2, "O");
    board.putSymbol(2, 4, "X");
    board.putSymbol(3, 4, "O");
    board.putSymbol(3, 3, "X");
    board.putSymbol(1, 2, "O");
    board.putSymbol(4, 2, "X");
    board.putSymbol(5, 3, "O");
    board.putSymbol(5, 1, "X");
    board.print();
    assertEquals("X", board.getWinner());
}

@Test
public void whenIsDrawThenReturnTrue() {
    board.setSize(3);
    board.putSymbol(1, 1, "X");
    board.putSymbol(1, 2, "O");
```

```java
    board.putSymbol(3, 2, "X");
    board.putSymbol(2, 2, "X");
    board.putSymbol(3, 3, "O");
    board.putSymbol(2, 1, "O");
    board.putSymbol(1, 3, "X");
    board.putSymbol(3, 1, "O");
    board.putSymbol(2, 3, "X");
    board.print();
    assertEquals("DRAW!", board.getWinner());
  }
}
```

```java
import org.junit.rules.ExpectedException;

import static org.junit.Assert.*;

public class UtilsTest {

  private Utils utils;

  @Before
  public void setUp() {
    utils = new Utils();
  }

  @Rule
  public ExpectedException thrownException
    = ExpectedException.none();

  @Test
  public void whenFileNotExistsThenThrowError()
    throws Exception {
    thrownException.expect(RuntimeException.class);
    utils.loadFile("board2.txt");
  }

  @Test
  public void whenFileExistsThenReturnContent()
    throws Exception {
    String content = utils.loadFile("symbols.txt");
    assertNotNull(content);
  }

  @Test
  public void whenGetBoardSizeIs11ThenThrowError()
    throws Exception {
    thrownException.expect(RuntimeException.class);
    utils.getBoardSize("11");
  }
```

```java
@Test
public void whenGetBoardSizeIs4ThenReturnSize()
  throws Exception {
  String content = utils.loadFile("board.txt");
  assertEquals(4, utils.getBoardSize(content));
}

@Test
public void whenGetSymbolsIsNotThreeThenThrowError()
  throws Exception {
  thrownException.expect(RuntimeException.class);
  utils.getSymbols("A,B,C,D");
}

@Test
public void whenSymbolsIsThreeThenReturnValues()
  throws Exception {
  String content = utils.loadFile("symbols.txt");
  String[] symbols = utils.getSymbols(content);
  assertArrayEquals(new String[]{"X","O","A"}, symbols);
}

@Test
public void whenInputFromConsoleIsWrongThrowException()
  throws Exception {
  thrownException.expect(RuntimeException.class);
  utils.getInputFromConsole("");
}

@Test
public void inputFromConsoleIsWrongFormatThrowException()
  throws Exception {
  thrownException.expect(RuntimeException.class);
  utils.getInputFromConsole("10");
}

@Test
public void inputFromConsoleThenReturnInput()
  throws Exception {
  Input input = utils.getInputFromConsole("2,3");
  assertEquals(2, input.getX());
  assertEquals(3, input.getY());
}
}
```

Appendices

A. Big O Notation

Big O Notation is a mathematical function, which helps us to analyze how complex an algorithm is in time and space. It matters when we build an application for millions of users. We implement different algorithms to solve one problem and measure how efficient is one respect to the other ones.

Time and Space complexity

Time complexity is related to how many steps take the algorithm.
Space complexity is related to how efficient the algorithm is using the memory and disk.
Both terms depend on the input size, the number of items in the input. We can analyze the complexity based on three cases:

- Best case or Big Omega **Ω(n)**: Usually, the algorithm executes in one step independently of the input size.
- Average case or Big Theta **Θ(n)**: When the input size is random
- Worst-case or Big O Notation **O(n)**: Gives us an upper bound on the runtime for any input. It gives us a kind of guarantee that the algorithm will never take any longer with new input size.

Order of growth

The order of growth is related to how the runtime of an algorithm increases when the size of the input increases without limit and tells us how efficient the algorithm is. We can compare the relative performance of alternative algorithms.

Common order-of-growth classifications:

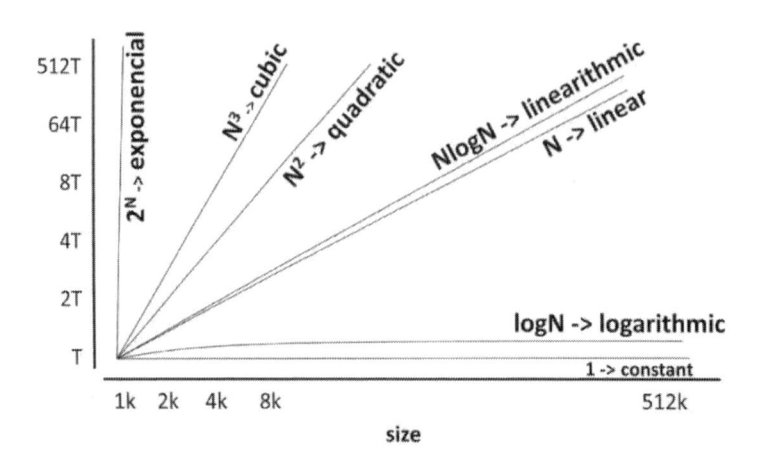

Figure A.1 Big O Notation - order of growth

Big O Notations examples:

O(1) - Constant

It does not matter if the input contains 1000 or 1 million items. The code always executes in one step.

```java
public class BigONotation {

  public void constant(List<String> list, String item) {
    list.add(item);
  }
}


@Test
public void test_constantTime() {
  List<String> list =
     new ArrayList<>(Arrays.asList("one", "two", "three"));
  bigONotation.constant(list, "four");
}
```

O(N) – linear

We say our algorithm runs in O(N) time if the number of steps depends on the number of items included in the input

```java
public int sum(int[] numbers) {
  int sum =0;
  for (int i =0; i<numbers.length; i++) {
    sum+=numbers[i];
  }
  return sum;
}


@Test
public void test_linearTime() {
  final int[] numbers = {1, 2, 4, 6, 1, 6};
  assertTrue(bigONotation.sum(numbers) == 20);
}
```

$O(N^2)$ – quadratic

When we have two loops nested in our code, we say that it's running in quadratic time $O(N^2)$. For example, when a 2D matrix is initialized in a tic-tac-toe game.

```java
private String [][] board;


public void initializeBoard(int size) {
  this.board = new String[size][size];
  for (int x = 0; x < size; x++) {
    for (int y = 0; y < size; y++) {
      board[x][y] = " ";
    }
  }
}


@Test
public void test_quadraticTime() {
  bigONotation.initializeBoard(3);
}
```

$O(N^3)$ - Cubic

We say that our algorithm runs in Cubic time when the code includes at the most three nested loops. For example, given N integers, how many triples sum to precisely zero? One approach (not the best) is to use three nested loops.

```java
public int countThreeSum(int[] numbers) {
  int N =numbers.length;
  int count =0;
  for (int i = 0; i<N; i++)
    for (int j = i+1; j<N; j++)
      for (int k = j+1; k<N; k++)
        if (numbers[i] + numbers[j] + numbers[k] == 0)
          count++;
  return count;
}


@Test
public void test_countThreeSum() {
  final int[] numbers = {30, -40, -20, -10, 40, 0, 10, 5};
  assertTrue(bigONotation.countThreeSum(numbers) == 4);
}
```

O(LogN) – logarithmic

This kind of algorithm produces a growth curve that peaks at the beginning and slowly flattens out as the size of the input increase.

$Log_2 8 = 3$
$Log_2 16 = 4$
$Log_2 32 = 5$

The binary search uses at most LogN key compares to search in a sorted array of size N. With 8 elements, takes 3 comparisons, with 16 elements takes 4 comparisons, with 32 elements takes 5 comparisons, and so on.

The complexity of an algorithm

To find the Big O complexity of an algorithm follows the following rules:

- Ignore the lower order terms
- Drop the leading constants

Example: If the time complexity of an algorithm is $2n^3 + 4n + 3$. Its Big O complexity simplifies to $O(n^3)$.

How to find the time complexity of an algorithm

Given the following algorithm:

```
public Integer sumEvenNumbers(Integer N) {
  int sum = 0;
  for (int number = 1; number <= N; number++)
    if ((number % 2) == 0)
      sum = sum + number;

  return sum;
}
```

First, we split the code into individual operations and then compute how many times it is being executed, as is shown in the following table.

Operation	Number of executions
int sum = 0;	1
int number = 1;	1
number <= N;	N

`number++`	N
`if ((number % 2) == 0)`	N
`sum = sum + number;`	N
`return sum;`	1

Now, we need to sum how many times each operation is executing.

Time complexity = 1 + 1 + N + N + N + N + 1 => 4N + 3

Why Big O Notation ignores constants?

Big O Notation describes how many steps are required relative to the number of data elements. And it serves as a way to classify the long-term growth rate of algorithms.
For instance, for *all amounts* of data, O(N) will be faster than O(N²), as shown in Figure A.2.

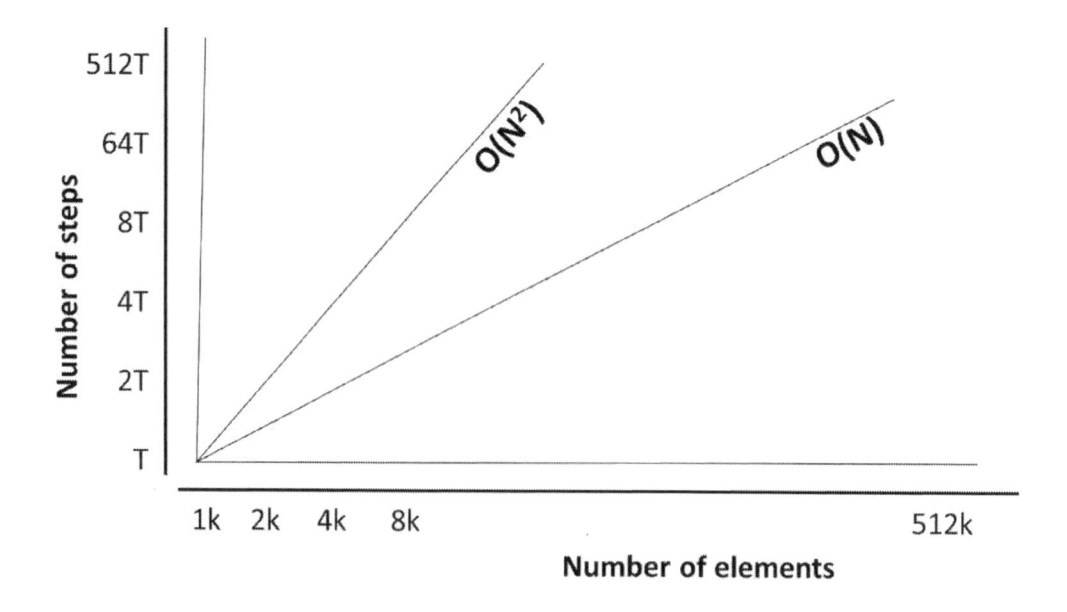

Figure A.2 O(N) is faster than O(N²) for all amounts of data

Now, if we compare O(100N) with O(N²), we can see that O(N²) is faster than O(100N) for some amounts of data, as shown in Figure A.3.

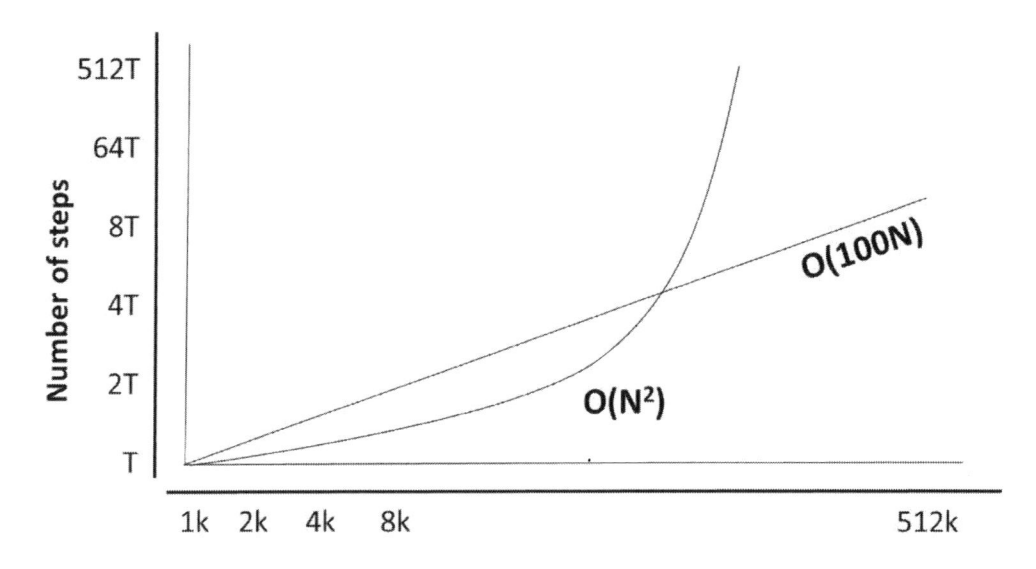

Figure A.3 O(N²) is faster than O(100N) for some amounts of data

But after a point, O(100N) becomes faster and remains faster for all increasing amounts of data from that point onward. And that is the reason why Big O Notation ignores constants. Because of this, O(100N) is written as O(N).

Printed in Great Britain
by Amazon